Growing Vegetables & Fruit
Around the Year

Growing Vegetables & Fruit Around the Year

A calendar of monthly tasks for the kitchen garden,
with over 300 photographs and 80 step-by-step techniques

Jonathan Edwards and Peter McHoy

southwater

This edition is published by Southwater, an imprint of Anness Publishing Ltd

Hermes House, 88–89 Blackfriars Road, London SE1 8HA

tel. 020 7401 2077; fax 020 7633 9499

www.southwaterbooks.com; www.annesspublishing.com

If you like the images in this book and would like to investigate using them for publishing, promotions or advertising, please visit our website www.practicalpictures.com for more information.

UK agent: The Manning Partnership Ltd; tel. 01225 478444; fax 01225 478440; sales@manning-partnership.co.uk

UK distributor: Grantham Book Services Ltd; tel. 01476 541080; fax 01476 541061; orders@gbs.tbs-ltd.co.uk

North American agent/distributor: National Book Network; tel. 301 459 3366; fax 301 429 5746; www.nbnbooks.com

Australian agent/distributor: Pan Macmillan Australia; tel. 1300 135 113; fax 1300 135 103; customer.service@macmillan.com.au

New Zealand agent/distributor: David Bateman Ltd; tel. (09) 415 7664; fax (09) 415 8892

ETHICAL TRADING POLICY

Because of our ongoing ecological investment programme, you, as our customer, can have the pleasure and reassurance of knowing that a tree is being cultivated on your behalf to naturally replace the materials used to make the book you are holding. For further information about this scheme, go to www.annesspublishing.com/trees

Publisher: Joanna Lorenz

Editorial Director: Judith Simons

Project Editors: Molly Perham and Sarah Uttridge

Assistant Editor: Lindsay Kaubi

Designer: Nigel Partridge

Cover Design: Balley Design Associates

Photographers: Peter Anderson, Jonathan Buckley, Sarah Cuttle, Paul Forrester, John Freeman, Michelle Garrett, Jacqui Hurit, Debbie Patterson and Steven Wooster

Editorial Reader: Penelope Goodare

Production Controller: Claire Rae

Material in this book has previously been published in *Gardening Through the Year*

NOTES

Bracketed terms are intended for American readers.

PUBLISHER'S NOTE

Although the advice and information in this book are believed to be accurate and true at the time of going to press, neither the authors nor the publisher can accept any legal responsibility or liability for any errors or omissions that may be made.

Contents

Introduction

Two of the keys to successful vegetable and fruit growing are to carry out tasks in the right way and at the correct time. Whether it's sowing or planting, training or feeding, harvesting or storing, each needs to be carried out at a particular time according to the types of plants you are growing and their stage of development. The weather patterns have changed in recent years so that seasons seem less distinct than they used to be, which makes getting the timing right more difficult. Divided into four sections, this book sets out the most important tasks for each season. Using step-by-step photographs, techniques are illustrated in detail so that they are straightforward to carry out, even for a gardening novice.

Planning ahead
Having all the main garden tasks mapped out through the seasons enables you to plan ahead so that you can make the most of your garden and available time. This is particularly important during the mad spring rush, when it seems that everything needs to be done at once. But don't be guided by the calendar alone, since the exact timing for each task will vary from year to year depending on the prevailing weather conditions as well as the local climate and soil in your garden. For example, if your soil is heavy it can be difficult to work and often remains colder for longer in spring, so that cultivation, sowing and planting will have to be delayed until the soil conditions improve.

You can keep herbs in production all year round if you have somewhere frost-free to keep them growing during the winter.

Plentiful harvests of vegetable and fruit crops bring the successful growing season to a close, and the main task now is to store the harvest correctly for use during the winter months.

Similarly, if your garden is exposed to cold winds or receives little sun, or perhaps lies in a frost pocket, you may have to adjust your timings by several weeks during spring and autumn to ensure success – putting off jobs during the early part of the year and advancing them at the end. Even if your garden has an average soil with moderate local climate you would be well advised to keep a close eye on how the seasons develop through the year and use this book as a general guide for timing – making adjustments as necessary.

During critical times such as early spring and autumn it's worth checking the local weather forecast each day so that you can take action if required. Simple but effective remedies, such as protecting vulnerable early sowings or newly planted tender plants from an unseasonally late frost in spring by covering them with a double layer of garden fleece or sheets of newspaper, might be all that's required to save the day.

Watering, weeding, and pest and disease control are the main summer tasks in a productive vegetable garden.

Though strawberries can be grown very successfully outdoors, if grown under glass they will provide an early harvest.

Around the year

Preparation starts in early spring for the sowing and planting season ahead. Early crops will need protecting for best results, especially in colder areas. By mid-spring a wide range of vegetables and herbs can be sown and planted if the weather and soil conditions allow. Further sowings of vegetables can be made as required over the coming months and by late spring tender crops can be planted out once the threat of frost has passed. The earliest salad crops will be ready for harvest at the end of the spring along with early potatoes.

By early summer, the main tasks are weeding and watering. You can also take steps to prevent pests by putting up barriers and traps. Summer is the time to prune many fruit bushes as well as plums and cherries to help prevent the spread of disease. Trained forms of fruit tree will also need pruning. Harvesting and storing of fruit, vegetables and herbs starts in earnest during the middle of the summer and continues right into the autumn in a well-planned garden.

As the dormant season closes in, you can extend the harvest period by protecting outdoor crops. Herbs can also be potted up for use during the winter months. And it's the best time to tackle many pruning jobs in the fruit garden as well as carrying out planned improvements and planting new specimens. The dormant season is also an ideal time to take stock of your successes and failures over the past year, as well as ordering new plants and seeds – making your choices according to how well the plants have performed so far in your garden.

Spring

With lengthening days and the air less chilly, early spring is the time when gardeners can't wait to start sowing and planting. It is also a time for caution, however, as winter seldom comes to a convenient end as spring approaches. A common cause of disappointment for novice gardeners is sowing too early – especially outdoors. Often, seeds and plants put out several weeks later in the season overtake ones planted earlier because they do not receive a check to growth. If you have the facilities you can make sowings indoors in pots and trays and plant the seedlings out when conditions are favourable a few weeks later. Some vegetables are not worth sowing early, because they mature quickly and later sowings will be ready for harvest at the same time as the riskier early sowings. By mid-spring many vegetables can be sown direct into a prepared seed bed. Popular crops such as lettuce, peas, radishes, spring onions (scallions), carrots, beetroot (beet), cauliflowers, spinach, summer cabbage and onions can all be sown now.

Growing herbs in pots means you can keep them close to the kitchen door so they are easy to pick when needed.

Preparing the vegetable plot

Before sowing and planting start in earnest, the vegetable plot needs to be carefully prepared. As soon as weather and soil conditions allow, areas that were dug over in autumn can be cleared of weeds and raked level. Light, sandy soils can be cultivated from scratch now, but heavier soils will need to have large clods broken down by frost–thaw action over the winter months. You could work from short boards or planks laid on the surface to spread your weight and prevent damage to the structure of heavy soils. Wait until the soil is dry enough not to stick to your tools and boots.

Improving the soil

Break down any remaining clods of soil, removing large stones and other debris as you go. If you are creating a seedbed, the surface needs to be as flat and even as possible, with the surface layer of soil having a fine, breadcrumb-like structure. If the soil is too wet to prepare, cover an area to be used for early sowings with a

It is essential to improve the soil before sowing or planting. Not only will you get bigger yields, but the crops will be less susceptible to pest and disease attacks too.

APPLYING FERTILIZER MANUALLY

1 If you are applying by hand, measure out the amount of fertilizer required for a square metre/yard, so that you can visualize how much you need, or pour it into a container as a measure and mark how full it is.

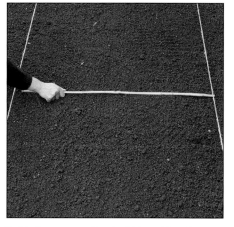

2 Mark out metre/yard widths with strings, then use a couple of canes to divide these into squares. When one square has been applied, move the back cane forwards to mark out the next area.

3 Use your measure to scoop up the appropriate amount of fertilizer, then sprinkle it evenly. It is a good idea to wear gloves when handling the fertilizer. Hold your hand about 15–23cm (6–9in) above the soil.

4 Always rake the fertilizer into the surface. This spreads it more evenly and helps it to penetrate more rapidly. Remove any stones or other debris brought to the surface by raking to leave the surface as even as possible.

piece of clear plastic sheeting. This will help to warm it up and dry it out by protecting it from further rains as well as encouraging surface weed seeds to germinate so they can be hoed off before sowing starts. Once the seedbed has been prepared, cover it with cloches or a sheet of clear plastic until you are ready to sow. The plastic will act like a mini-greenhouse – warming the soil and so speeding germination and seedling establishment. If cats are a problem in your area but you don't want to keep the rain off, cover the prepared vegetable plot with netting to prevent them from digging and fouling the seedbed.

The vegetable plot also needs regular feeding if yields are not to suffer. Unlike beds and borders in the ornamental garden, little natural recycling occurs. The crops are removed and leaves do not naturally fall and decay. Bulky organic manures

USING GARDEN FLEECE

1 Sow the seeds and cover the area with the fleece. It will help warm the soil, and protect seedlings from a degree or two of frost and from flying insect pests. Anchor it down loosely with bricks while you secure the edges.

2 You can secure the edges by burying them in a slit cut into the ground or just heaping soil over them. Water will soak through the fleece, and it will also stretch as the seedlings emerge and develop into sturdy plants.

3 You can buy various types of proprietary pegs to hold the fleece in position, and these are preferable to soil because they make it easier to lift and replace the fleece for weeding and other cultivation tasks.

do much to improve soil structure and increase the nutrient-holding capabilities of the soil, but unless you follow an intensive organic approach and apply sufficient manures and garden compost, some chemical fertilizers are necessary if you want a heavy crop. The quickest way to apply a general fertilizer to the whole vegetable plot is with a wheeled spreader that you can adjust to deliver the appropriate amount. Calculate and test the delivery rate first over polythene laid on the patio or lawn.

Protecting early crops

Horticultural fleece was unknown to a previous generation of gardeners, but the fact that it is now widely used commercially is evidence of its usefulness. The fleece warms up the soil like a cloche, while allowing rain to penetrate, and should provide protection from a degree or two of frost. It also acts as a barrier against flying insect pests that are now beginning to be active. You can use it just to start off your seeds or as protection for a growing crop.

Other types of protective covers can also be used. Insect-proof mesh

is a very fine, long-lasting net, which effectively keeps out flying insect pests. Although it doesn't provide frost protection, it can be used to protect crops from late spring onwards when garden fleece holds in too much heat and cannot be used. Perforated plastic films, known as

floating cloches, let through rain and 'give' enough to rise with the growing crop.

Whichever crop protection you use, you will have to pull it back to weed and thin plants. You will find that weeds thrive under the protection as well as the crops!

Broad (fava) beans, like most vegetables, need an open sunny site which is protected from strong winds, and a reasonably fertile soil.

Early planting and sowing

Sowing early can be a gamble. If the weather is cold the seeds may rot before they germinate, and some vegetables tend to run to seed if they are subject to very cold conditions after germinating. The exact timing will vary from year to year, depending on the prevailing soil and weather conditions. In some years, in some gardens, the soil temperature may not rise high enough until mid- or late spring.

Making a start

If you intend to make a lot of early sowings or your soil is cold and heavy, consider investing in a soil thermometer to check the temperature. Insert the thermometer to a depth of 5–7.5cm (2–3in) each day and record the temperature. Wait until it has risen above 5°C (41°F) for a week before you sow broad (fava) beans and peas, and above 7°C (45°F) for most other early crops. You can help to boost the soil temperature by covering the seedbed with cloches or a sheet of plastic.

If you are sowing early for the first time, concentrate on hardy crops, such as broad beans and early peas.

Sowing planner

Crop	Temperature	Timing
Bean, broad (fava)	5°C (41°F)	late winter – early spring
Bean, French (green)	10°C (50°F)	mid-spring – early summer
Bean, runner	10°C (50°F)	mid-spring – early summer
Beetroot (beet)	7°C (45°F)	late winter – early summer
Broccoli	5°C (41°F)	mid-spring – late spring
Brussels sprout	5°C (41°F)	late winter – mid-spring
Cabbage	5°C (41°F)	early spring – late spring
Calabrese	5°C (41°F)	late winter – late spring
Carrot	7°C (45°F)	early spring – early summer
Cauliflower	5°C (41°F)	late winter – mid-spring
Celery	10°C (50°F)	early spring – mid-spring
Corn	10°C (50°F)	mid-spring – late spring
Courgette (zucchini)	15°C (59°F)	mid-spring – late spring
Cucumber	15°C (59°F)	early spring – mid-spring
Leek	7°C (45°F)	late winter – mid-spring
Lettuce	5°C (41°F)	late winter – early summer
Marrow	15°C (59°F)	mid-spring – late spring
Onion	7°C (45°F)	late winter – early spring
Parsnip	7°C (45°F)	late winter – mid-spring
Pea	5°C (41°F)	late winter – late spring
Pepper	15°C (59°F)	early spring – mid-spring
Radish	5°C (41°F)	midwinter – late summer
Spinach	10°C (50°F)	early spring – early summer
Swede (rutabaga)	5°C (41°F)	early spring – early summer
Tomato	15°C (59°F)	early spring – mid-spring
Turnip	5°C (41°F)	early spring – early summer

SOWING EARLY VEGETABLES OUTDOORS

1 Peas and broad (fava) beans are best sown in multiple rows so that they can support each other as they grow, with walking space between the double or triple rows. Take out a flat-bottomed drill 5–8cm (2–3in) deep.

2 Space the seeds by hand. Peas should be planted 4–8cm (1½–3in) apart in three staggered rows, and broad beans should be 23cm (9in) apart in a double staggered row.

3 Pull the soil back over the drill to cover the seeds. If the ground is dry, water well, and keep watering as they grow. If seed-eaters, such as mice or birds, are a problem, netting or traps may be necessary.

PLANTING ONION SETS

1 Take out a shallow drill with the corner of a hoe or rake. To keep the drill straight, use a garden line held on pegs driven into the ground at each end of the row. Plant the sets about 15cm (6in) apart.

2 Pull the soil back over the drill, but leave the tips of the onions protruding. If birds are a problem – they may try to pull the onions out by the wispy old stems – protect them with netting.

Dividing chives

Herbaceous herbs, such as chives, are best divided in early spring or autumn. Use a fork to loosen the soil under the clump and break it up into suitable sized pieces for replanting.

1 When dividing in early spring, cut down the tops to leave 2.5cm (1in) so that you can see what you are doing and to make the clump easy to divide.

2 Having cut off the tops, tease the clump apart carefully with your hands, avoiding root damage as far as possible. Divide the pieces until each division has 10–20 stems. Make sure each has a generous root system.

3 Replant the divisions in prepared ground, spacing them 25cm (10in) apart. Water well and keep well watered until they are established.

You could also try a few short rows of a wider range of vegetables, but be prepared to resow if they don't do well. In unfavourable conditions peas and beans can be sown in containers in a coldframe to plant out as seedlings. Alternatively, sow seed in a piece of guttering filled with compost (soil mix) that can be transferred to the garden as a complete row of seedlings. Early crops of brassicas, beetroot (beets) and carrots can also be started off in pots – sow thinly and thin seedlings to leave six of the strongest in each pot. Plant out when the soil and weather conditions improve, spacing the plants about 15cm (6in) apart.

Hardy vegetables, such as broad beans and brassicas, that were sown in the greenhouse or coldframe during late winter should be growing well and forming sturdy plants by early spring. When soil and weather conditions allow these can be planted out, after they have been hardened off and acclimatized to the harsher conditions outdoors. Position cloches over the planting site to warm the soil while the plants are being hardened off. Plant out at the correct planting distance and water well before re-covering with the cloches.

Onions and shallots can also be planted now. The biggest onions are usually grown from seed, but the results can be disappointing. Sets (small onion bulbs) are an almost foolproof way to grow onions and shallots, and you should be rewarded with a reasonable crop for very little effort. Shallots are spaced about 15cm (6in) apart, so that the tip of the bulb is just protruding. Pull the soil back round them with a hoe or rake. Shallots are useful for an early crop, and you can usually plant them outdoors in late winter, except in very cold regions. If you missed the winter planting, start them off in individual pots now. Keep the pots in a coldframe or greenhouse until the shoots are 2.5–5cm (1–2in) high. Then plant the sprouted shallots in the garden, spacing them about 15cm (6in) apart in the row.

Sowing early vegetables under cover

In early spring many vegetables can be started off in a greenhouse, a coldframe or a propagator. Once they have germinated, you will need the space and facilities for pricking out the seedlings and potting them on. Ideally you need to maintain a temperature of 15–19°C (60–66°F) – lower temperatures will slow establishment and growth. The aim is to provide the best possible growing environment in which the plants can grow and develop without suffering a check in growth. Wait until mid-spring before you sow courgettes (zucchini), and French (green) and runner beans.

Conditions for germination

All seeds need air, warmth and moisture to germinate and some need light too. How quickly and evenly they germinate will depend on how well you can control these conditions as well as the type and condition of the seed you use. Seeds will not germinate if the tempature is too high or too low. How old the seed is as well as the conditions in which it was stored will also affect its viability to germinate. Check the seed packets for the recommended sowing temperature and depth.

A coldframe with a soil bed can be used for growing winter and early spring vegetables. Coldframes with solid walls made from brick retain heat and provide much better protection.

When sowing under cover, there are a few golden rules you should follow:
• Use fresh, well-sterilized sowing compost (soil mix). Don't use ordinary potting compost because this contains too many nutrients, which will damage the emerging roots.
• Sieve the compost to remove lumps. This is particularly important for small-seeded varieties.
• Firm the compost lightly with a

special tamper or the bottom of another container to remove air pockets and level the compost.
• Water the compost before sowing by standing the pot or seed tray in a shallow tray of water until the surface of the compost darkens with moisture. Continue watering by this method as the seedlings emerge.
• Sow the seed evenly over the surface, with plenty of space between

SOWING IN TRAYS

1 Fill the seed tray with a good quality seed compost (soil mix), spread it evenly and remove any lumps. Tamp down the compost lightly to produce a level surface. Sow the seed thinly across the compost.

2 Cover with a thin layer of compost (unless the seeds are very fine or need light to germinate), lightly firm down and label the tray. Labelling is very important because many seedlings look the same.

SOWING IN CELLULAR TRAYS

Fill the blocks with compost (soil mix) and tap on the table to settle it down. Sow one or two seeds in each cell. Cover lightly with compost. Remove the weaker seedling from each cell if both germinate.

USING A PROPAGATOR

1 Place the seed trays in a propagator. Adjust the temperature of heated propagators – you should find the optimum temperature on the packet. You may need to compromise if different seeds need different temperatures.

2 If the propagator is unheated, it should be kept in a warm position in a greenhouse or even somewhere well lit within the house. Start opening the vents once the seeds have germinated to start the hardening-off process.

Multiple sowing

Many root crops, including beetroot (beets) and turnips as well as onions, shallots and leeks, can be sown in pots and planted out in clusters. Sow six to eight seeds in an 8cm (3in) pot filled with fresh compost and reduce the number of seedlings to six by removing the weakest. Grow on and harden off as normal and plant out at double the recommended spacing for individual plants. The plants will naturally push apart as they grow and produce a good crop of roots or bulbs. This method not only reduces the amount of space they take up in the greenhouse and coldframe but also cuts down on the time it takes to grow them and plant them out, as well as minimizing the cost by using fewer pots and less compost. Since the whole potful of plants is set out as one, there is less root disturbance which helps to avoid a check in growth. This is a useful way of growing mini-vegetables, which have become popular.

each seed. This will make pricking out and potting on the seedlings a lot easier later.

• Cover the pots or seed trays with a clear plastic lid and put them in a warm position out of direct sunlight, or place them in a propagator. Alternatively, you can cover the pots loosely with clear plastic bags. Those that require dark can be put into an airing cupboard until they show the first signs of germination.

• Move seedlings to a well-lit spot away from draughts and shaded from strong direct sunlight after they have germinated, and prick them out once they produce their true leaves.

Sowing small seed

Very fine seed is much more difficult to sow evenly than larger seed. You can overcome this by mixing it with a small amount of dry silver sand before you sow. Not only will the sand effectively 'dilute' the fine seed, allowing you to spread it more evenly, but you can also see where you have already sown because the light-coloured sand stands out against the dark-coloured compost.

Pricking out

Once seedlings are large enough to handle they can be pricked out into cellular trays. Each plant will have its

own pocket of soil, separated from the others, and there will be less root disturbance when the plants are transplanted into the garden. Water the fresh compost a few hours before you begin pricking out, and keep the seedlings moist with a mist sprayer.

PRICKING OUT

1 Loosen the seedlings in the tray before pricking out, and lift them one at a time by their seed leaves – the first ones to open when the seed germinates – supporting the roots with the end of a pencil or dibber.

2 Make a hole large enough to take the roots. Gently firm the compost around the roots, being careful not to press too hard. Water thoroughly through a fine rose, then keep the plants our of direct sunlight for a few days.

SOWING IN DEGRADABLE POTS

For plants that dislike root disturbance, it may be worthwhile to sow them in pots made of peat or some other degradable material. The entire pot can then be planted directly into the ground.

Growing vegetables from seed

Vegetable sowing begins in earnest in mid-spring, with crops like beetroot (beets), spinach beet, summer cabbages, salad and pickling onions, scorzonera and turnips, as well as further sowings of lettuces, peas, radishes, spinach, carrots and cauliflowers. Dwarf beans can be sown in mild areas. There are several ways in which you can grow vegetables in the garden: in rows or beds, among other plants or as part of a formal but decorative potager.

Designing the plot

Traditionally, vegetables have been grown in straight rows in a dedicated area of the garden with paths between rows. This arrangement means that you can choose the most suitable part of the garden to grow your crops and you can prepare the soil to benefit the crops you are growing. Moreover, by growing in straight rows it is easier to tell your plants from weeds – which is particularly important when they are at the seedling stage. The main drawbacks are that there is a lot of competition among plants in the row when they reach maturity and a lot of space is wasted between the rows.

By growing in dedicated beds, the middle of which is just within reach from permanent paths that run along the sides, you can grow crops in shorter straight rows. Because there are fewer paths, this system is more space-efficient, and the closer spacing between rows means there is less room for weeds to get established. You do not have to walk on the soil, which means it is not compacted and so remains in better condition. Resulting crops are of better quality and grow more quickly than in the traditional row system. You can improve growing conditions further by making raised beds.

Not everyone has the space for a vegetable plot, and you can also grow vegetables among ornamental plants. The main disadvantages to this are that the vegetables suffer from more competition for light, nutrients and moisture, they are more difficult to look after, and they leave gaps in the display when they are harvested. However, because the plants are not all growing in one place, pest and disease outbreaks are likely to be less common. You can either hide your crops away at the back of ornamental borders or make a display of the more decorative vegetables, such as frilly-leaved lettuce and brightly coloured chard, which make an edible alternative to summer bedding. In a formal garden you could grow vegetables in beds edged with low-growing box in the style of a traditional French potager.

Perennial vegetables, such as asparagus, rhubarb and artichokes, are normally grown in an area away from the annual crops where they can be left undisturbed and cropped at appropriate times of the year.

FLUID SOWING

1 Sow the seeds thickly on damp kitchen paper and keep them in a warm place to germinate. Make sure that they remain moist and check daily to monitor germination.

2 Once the roots emerge, and before the leaves open, wash the seeds into a sieve and mix them into prepared wallpaper paste (without fungicide) or a special sowing gel.

3 Mark a straight line using a length of garden twine held on pegs driven into the ground, then take out the drill in the normal way, with the corner of a hoe or rake.

4 Fill a plastic bag with the paste and cut off one corner (rather like an icing bag). Twist the top of the bag to prevent the paste oozing out, then move along the row as you squeeze out the seeds in the paste.

SOWING MAINCROP VEGETABLES OUTDOORS

1 Rake the seedbed level and remove any stones or other debris that come to the surface. Make sure that all perennial weeds are removed.

2 Most vegetables grown in rows, such as beetroots and carrots, are best sown in drills. Always use a garden line to make sure the drills – and therefore the rows – are straight.

3 Take out a shallow drill with the corner of a hoe or rake. Always refer to the seed packet for the recommended sowing depth of the seed, which varies considerably.

4 Flood the drills with water a few minutes before sowing if the weather is dry. Watering after sowing is likely to wash the seeds away or into clumps.

5 Sprinkle the seeds thinly and evenly along the drill. Do this carefully now and you will save time later: you will have to thin the seedlings if they have been sown too close.

6 Use a rake to return soil to the drills by raking in the direction of the row and not across it, otherwise you might spread the seeds and produce an uneven row.

Seed types

Most vegetable seed is bought in packets that contain a foil sachet. You can also get pelleted seed that has been coated in clay. This is easier to sow evenly and at the correct depth. The clay simply falls away when it becomes moist. A few types of popular vegetables are supplied embedded at the correct spacing on a strip of degradable material (see left). A few difficult-to-germinate varieties can be bought 'primed': in these cases the first germination stage has been reached. All these preparations are an expensive way to buy seeds, but save much time and disappointment.

Alternatively, you could improve your chances of success with difficult seeds by fluid sowing, which involves germinating the seeds before sowing. Parsnips, early carrots, onions and parsley are sometimes sown this way.

Stony soil

If the soil is very stony, it is worth making an effort to remove stones from small areas of ground before planting certain crops. Root crops, such as carrots and parsnips in particular, need a clear root-run, otherwise they will produce poor quality, forked and stunted roots that are less useful in the kitchen.

SOWING ROOT CROPS IN STONY SOIL

1 To create the perfect root-run in stony ground use a crowbar to make conical holes at the required planting distance.

2 Fill each hole with potting compost (soil mix). Sow the seed in the centre before covering with more soil.

Planting vegetables

Cabbages and cauliflowers are not normally sown in their final positions. Instead, they are started off in a seedbed, or sown in late winter and spring in pots or modules in the greenhouse, then transplanted to their growing positions. If you are unable to grow your own plants from seed, you can order a limited number of cultivars by mail order from seed companies. Alternatively, buy young plants from garden centres from mid-spring, which can be a useful way of replacing losses or filling gaps.

Dealing with young plants

It is always best to raise your own plants from seed. Buying plants is more expensive than buying seed, and inevitably you will have far less choice of varieties. If you do buy plants from a garden centre, check to find out when they are going to have their next delivery and buy as soon as they arrive. Look for named varieties that are stocky and well

TRANSPLANTING CABBAGES AND CAULIFLOWERS

1 If you have your own seedlings to transplant into the vegetable patch – perhaps growing in a coldframe – water thoroughly an hour before you lift them if the soil is dry.

2 Loosen the soil with a fork or trowel. It is best to lift each one individually with a trowel if possible, but if they have not been thinned sufficiently this may be difficult.

3 Plant with a trowel and firm the soil well. A convenient way to firm soil around the roots is to insert the blade of the trowel about 5cm (2in) away from the plant and press it firmly towards the roots.

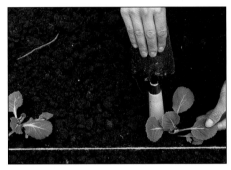

4 You can also firm the soil with the handle of the trowel if you don't want to use your hands, but this is not a good idea if the soil is wet as it will dirty the handle. Always water in thoroughly after transplanting.

Planting planner

Crop	Planting distances		Crop	Planting distances	
	Between rows	In the row		Between rows	In the row
Bean, broad (fava)	45cm (18in)	10cm (4in)	Leek	30cm (12in)	15cm (6in)
Bean, French (green)	45cm (18in)	10cm (4in)	Lettuce, hearting	30cm (12in)	30cm (12in)
Bean, runner	60cm (24in)	15cm (6in)	Lettuce, loose leaf	23cm (9in)	5cm (2in)
Broccoli	60cm (24in)	60cm (24in)	Marrow	90cm (36in)	90cm (36in)
Brussels sprouts	90cm (36in)	90cm (36in)	Onion, maincrop	23cm (9in)	5cm (2in)
Calabrese	30cm (12in)	15cm (6in)	Onion, salad	15cm (6in)	1cm (½in)
Cabbage, Chinese	45cm (18in)	30cm (12in)	Parsnip	23cm (9in)	15cm (6in)
Cabbage, spring	30cm (12in)	15cm (6in)	Pea	60cm (24in)	5cm (2in) in 15cm (6in) drill
Cabbage, summer	30cm (12in)	30cm (12in)	Pepper	45cm (18in)	45cm (18in)
Cabbage, winter	45cm (18in)	45cm (18in)	Potato, early	60cm (24in)	50cm (20in)
Carrot, early	15cm (6in)	5cm (2in)	Potato, maincrop	75cm (30in)	40cm (16in)
Cauliflower, summer	45cm (18in)	45cm (18in)	Shallot	30cm (12in)	23cm (9in)
Cauliflower, autumn	60cm (24in)	60cm (24in)	Spinach	30cm (12in)	15cm (6in)
Corn	35cm (14in)	35cm (14in)	Swede (rutabaga)	30cm (12in)	23cm (9in)
Courgette (zucchini)	90cm (36in)	90cm (36in)	Tomato	45cm (18in)	45cm (18in)
Garlic	23cm (9in)	10cm (4in)	Turnip	15cm (6in)	15cm (6in)

grown and that have dark leaves (where appropriate). Avoid any that look lanky or damaged or that are suffering from stress.

Transplanting inevitably causes a check in growth because the roots are disturbed and the plant has to acclimatize to its new, more exposed environment. However, there are a number of things you can do to minimize the disruption. Always transplant when the young plant has reached the right stage of growth and when weather and soil conditions allow. Carefully harden off plants raised under cover before transplanting them into the open. Ideally, water the plants before and after transplanting on a day when the weather is overcast and the soil

is moist. On sunny days, shade the transplants and keep them well watered until they are established. In general, younger plants transplant better than older ones do.

Prepare and mark out the planting site before you start, and transplant only a few plants at a time. Do not lift a whole row at once because delays in replanting will increase stress. Transplant only those young plants that look healthy and vigorous, discarding any weak and spindly ones. Use a measuring stick laid along the row with the planting distances marked on it as a guide to ensure correct spacing and speed up the transplanting process. Most transplants are planted at the same depth as they were growing in the

seedbed or container and gently firmed in. Leeks are the main exception to this rule and should be planted in 15cm (6in) deep holes and watered in instead of firmed.

Planting potatoes

It is now safe to plant potatoes in most areas, since it will take several weeks before the frost-sensitive shoots emerge from the soil, and these can be protected by earthing (hilling) up the plants. In cold areas, however, it is best to chit your potatoes and delay planting for a couple of weeks. Place the tubers in a tray in a light position, perhaps by a window, where there is no risk of frost. Chitting is useful if you want the tubers to get off to a quick start.

PLANTING POTATOES

1 Use a draw hoe, a spade or a rake head to make wide, flat-bottomed or V-shaped drills 10–13cm (4–5in) deep. Space the rows about 60cm (24in) apart for early varieties, and 75cm (30in) for the maincrop.

2 Space the tubers about 40–50cm (16–20in) apart in the rows. Make sure that the shoots or 'eyes' (buds about to grow into shoots) face upwards. For larger tubers, leave only three sprouts per plant and rub off the others.

3 Cover the tubers by pulling the excavated soil back into the drill. Do this carefully to avoid moving or damaging the tubers. Firm the soil with the back of the rake and water well.

4 If you don't want to earth (hill) up your potatoes (see page 31), plant under a black plastic sheet. Bury the edges in slits in the soil and cover with soil to anchor the sheet.

5 Make cross-shaped slits in the plastic with a knife where each tuber is to be planted. To make sure you get the correct spacing cut a piece of cane to use as a guide.

6 Plant through the slit, using a trowel. Make sure that the tuber is covered with 2.5–5cm (1–2in) of soil. The shoots will be able to find their way through the slits.

Protecting your crops

You will get bigger and better crops earlier in the year if you protect them from the worst of the weather, especially late frosts. A range of techniques is available that will help you protect vulnerable young plants from the weather as well as from pest and disease attacks. Practising good garden hygiene can also help to prevent problem pests and diseases, so that you do not have to resort to using chemical sprays.

Be vigilant

Most pests and diseases can be prevented from getting a foothold by keeping crops growing well. If your plants are vigorous and do not suffer from stress, such as a check in growth as the result of a shortage of water or nutrients, they will be able to shrug off most pest and disease attacks. Clearing away all dead or diseased material will also help to prevent problems being transferred from one crop to the next. At the end of the season, make sure that you throw away or burn

PROTECTING AGAINST LIGHT FROSTS

1 Newspaper makes an excellent temporary insulation against sudden frosts in spring. In the evening, drop several sheets over the susceptible crops, to create air pockets. Remove the paper during the day.

2 Garden fleece can also be used to provide protection against light frosts. It is very light and will not harm the plants. Unlike newspaper, it can be left on during the day since light penetrates through it.

any diseased material rather than composting it so that you do not reinfect plants the following year. One of the advantages of growing vegetables mixed among ornamental plants is that pests and diseases will be less likely to spread. In a dedicated vegetable plot, a crop rotation system, where different types of crop are grown in each area from year to year, will also help prevent problems occurring.

Stay vigilant at all times for the first signs of pest and disease outbreaks. If you can catch them early and take appropriate action, the plants may recover and go on to produce good crops.

Protection for early strawberries

Strawberries do not need protection from frost, but cloches will bring the crop on earlier and will also help to keep it clean and protect it from birds and other animals.

With regular watering, feeding and weeding, and watching carefully for any problems, you should be able to keep plants healthy without using chemicals against pests and diseases.

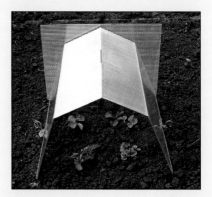

Cover the plants as soon as possible, but remember to leave access for pollinating insects when the plants are in flower. Most cloches have a system of ventilation that allows for this on warm days. With plastic tunnel cloches, lift the material along one side to allow for pollination.

Know your enemy

Most pests conform to a regular annual lifecycle which you can use to your advantage. By learning about potential pests you can predict when they are most likely to be a problem and take action to avoid them. Carrots sown by late spring, for example, will be harvested before the carrot fly pest is problematic, while peas sown before late spring or after late spring will not be in flower when the pea moth is around and so cannot be attacked. Potato blight is a serious problem in warm, wet weather, but early crops are less likely to be affected.

Using barriers

Barriers can be used to protect certain crops from particular pests. For example, when planting brassicas, such as cabbages and cauliflowers, you can protect them from egg-laying cabbage root fly by placing a felt collar around each plant. A 15cm (6in) square collar cut from a piece of old carpet underlay or roofing felt that's been slit to the centre can be positioned around each seedling after planting so that the female flies cannot lay eggs in the ground around the root.

You can protect rows of carrots from carrot fly by putting up a low fence of insect-proof mesh around your crop. These pests are known to fly very low and are unable to clear a barrier that is higher than about 75cm (30in). Other crops can be protected from flying pests using special crop covers. Cabbage-white butterflies, for example, can be kept off susceptible crops by covering rows with garden fleece. Lay the fabric loosely over the row so there is plenty of room for the plants to develop, and bury the edges to keep it safely in place.

Disease-resistant cultivars

Brussels sprout	powdery mildew	'Adonis', 'Cascade', 'Citadel', 'Cor', 'Icarus', 'Odette', 'Tavernos', 'Topline', 'Troika'
Cabbage	downy mildew	'Derby Day', 'Stonehead'
Calabrese	clubroot	'Trixie'
Courgette (zucchini)	mosaic virus	'Defender', 'Supremo'
Leeks	rust	'Bandit', 'Conora', 'Poribleu', 'Poristo'
Lettuce	downy mildew	'Avondefiance', 'Challenge', 'Dolly', 'Musette', 'Soraya'
Marrow (large zucchini)	mosaic virus	'Tiger Cross'
Parsnip	canker	'Arrow', 'Avonresister', 'Gladiator', 'Javelin', 'Lancer', 'White Gem'
Potato	blackleg	'Kestrel', 'Maxine', 'Pentland Crown', 'Saxon'
	blight	'Cara', 'Maris Piper', 'Pentland Dell', 'Romano', 'Stirling', 'Valor'
	virus	'Pentland Crown', 'Sante', 'Wilja'
	nematode	'Accent', 'Cara', 'Concorde', 'Maris Piper', 'Nadine', 'Pentland Javelin', 'Sante'

PROTECTING AGAINST PESTS

1 Larger crops can be protected from birds by using fine nets, which are held above the crop on special frames. Because they let through air and moisture, they can be left in place.

2 Wire mesh nets can be used to protect your crops against rodents and rabbits. Bury the edges well below the soil to prevent them digging underneath.

3 Fleece and insect-proof mesh can be used to protect growing crops from flying pests, such as cabbage-white butterflies. Use insect-proof mesh for summer crops.

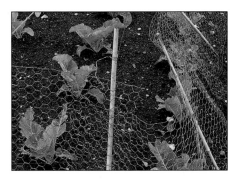

4 Cabbage root fly can be kept at bay by placing a felt or plastic collar around the base of the brassica plant in order to stop the fly laying its eggs.

Growing herbs

Every garden has the space to grow herbs. Many make ideal container plants because they are fairly drought tolerant, and you can even grow them in hanging baskets. Growing them in containers also means you can position the herbs in a convenient spot near to the kitchen. If you want to grow a lot of herbs, however, you will need to grow them in the garden either among other plants in mixed beds and borders or in a dedicated herb garden. If you are new to growing herbs, choose types that you use most often in the kitchen.

Siting a herb garden

Most herbs prefer a sunny site protected from cold winds, although a few, including chives, lovage and mint, can tolerate shadier conditions.

Position the herb garden as near to the kitchen as possible, so that it is convenient to collect herbs as and when they are needed. Herb gardens can make very decorative features if they are well planned (see below). Traditional herb wheels always look effective in any garden, but in a contemporary setting you might wish to consider one based on a chequer-board design with paving slabs as the 'white' squares and planting pockets filled with herbs as the 'black' squares.

The soil should be well-drained for most of the Mediterranean herbs. Prepare the site by digging it thoroughly and removing all weeds and other debris. Rake it level before you mark out the design that you want on the surface with sand trickled from a bottle or cup.

Stocking a herb garden

You can raise herbs from seeds or buy them as plants. Once you have a few plants established, you can also propagate your own from cuttings, division or layering, so a herb garden needn't cost a lot to create. Many herbs, once established, will spread themselves prolifically by seed or runners without any help from you. Indeed, mint is so invasive that most gardeners grow it in pots buried in the ground, to prevent it taking over. However, some herbs, such as parsley and basil, will prove expensive if you use a lot of them, unless grown from seed. On the other hand some, including golden and variegated forms of marjoram, mint, sage and thyme, do not come true from seed, so you will need to buy these as plants. Also bear in mind that annual

MAKING A HERB WHEEL

1 Use string and canes to mark a circle, then measure off a series of equal points on the circumference for the spokes. Sink a length of earthenware pipe in the centre.

2 Trace over the whole design with fine sand or line-marker paint. Although you can have as many sections as you like, more than six or eight will look fussy.

3 Excavate a trench for the bricks and fill it with dry concrete mix to form a firm footing. Remember that you want the top level of bricks to be level with the top of the earthenware pipe.

4 Build the outer circle and spokes with one or two courses of bricks, set in mortar. A herb wheel does not have to be very high; two or three courses of bricks should be sufficient.

5 Fill in the sections of the wheel and the earthenware pipe with a layer of rubble and gravel to provide drainage. Then add good-quality topsoil mixed with fine grit.

6 Plant up the herb wheel with a selection of culinary herbs, such as sage, thyme, rosemary and lemon verbena. Water in thoroughly and add an organic mulch.

PLANTING A HERB GARDEN

1 First prepare the site by thoroughly weeding and forking over to break up the soil, then rake the ground level. Box trees have been used to line this wooden-edged herb bed.

2 To help plan the planting, mark out the design with sand trickled out of a pot. If you make a mistake or change your mind you can easily replace the lines.

3 Remove the herbs from their pots and plant them carefully, making sure that they are at the same level as they were in the container, and loosening the rootball.

4 Water the plants thoroughly and keep them watered in dry weather until they are established. Avoid planting on a hot day; if possible, do it when rain is forecast.

5 The newly planted herb garden will look rather bare at first, but it won't be long before the plants begin to fill out and grow to fit their allocated space.

herbs will need to be replaced each year, and some perennial herbs will thrive for only a few years.

There are many herb specialists that stock a huge range of different cultivars, but for most circumstances you'll find a good range of basic (and most useful) herbs at your local garden centre. Look for stocky, well-grown plants with fresh foliage and no signs of pests or diseases. Some herbs are particularly prone to certain pests and diseases, so inspect the plants for symptoms. Mints, for example, often suffer from rust disease, which shows itself as tiny orange spots on the undersides of the leaves. Watch out for the tell-tale pale lines in the leaves of parsley that are an indication of celery fly attack, and inspect bay trees carefully for scale insects. Also check that the herbs have been hardened off properly before you buy. If not, you will have to do it yourself before you plant.

Grow herbs with similar requirements together, as this will make them easier to look after. Plant them at the same depth they were in their pots and don't forget to label them. It's also worth noting down the names of the herbs on your planting plan just in case the labels get mislaid. Water well until they are established.

You can grow herbs in almost any container from plastic pots to large tubs. For convenience, keep them near to the kitchen door.

Hardening off tender vegetables

The greenhouse is at its busiest during mid-spring with early sowings of vegetables to be hardened off before planting out and new sowings of tender plants to be made. The secret to making the best use of available space is careful planning. You can ease the pressure on space to some extent by erecting temporary staging and shelves to both sides of the greenhouse. If the greenhouse has all-glass sides, even the shelving under the staging can be put to good use. It's also worth investing in one or two coldframes to accommodate the overflow as the seedlings take up more space.

Planning and scheduling

First, work out exactly how many plants you think you will need in your garden and use this to calculate how many seeds to sow. A good general guide is to sow twice as many seeds as you need plants. This will then accommodate any losses and allow for a 70 per cent germination rate – the minimum standard for commercially produced vegetable seed and a reasonable expectation for commercial flower seed.

Because most seed packets contain hundreds if not thousands of seeds, a single packet will contain sufficient for several seasons. However, once

Ridge or outdoor cucumbers should be sown in the greenhouse in late spring and hardened off before being planted out in the garden.

SOWING TENDER VEGETABLES

1 Sow runner beans about six to eight weeks before the last frost is likely. Fill a 15–20cm (6–8in) pot with sowing compost to within 2.5cm (1in) of the rim. Put three seeds in the pot, cover with compost and water gently.

2 Keep the pots in a warm place, and give them good light as soon as the seeds have germinated. If all the seeds germinate, pull out the weakest seedlings to leave just one or two of the strongest to grow on.

3 Outdoor and greenhouse cucumbers can be sown now. Use small pots and fill with a seed-sowing compost to within 2.5cm (1in) of the rim. Position two or three seeds in each pot, placing them on their narrow edge. Cover with compost and water.

4 Corn is best raised in pots to plant out after the threat of frost has passed, except in very mild regions. You can use ordinary pots, but many gardeners prefer to use fibre pots. The roots will grow through these once they are planted out.

the foil pouch inside the seed packet has been opened, the viability of the seed deteriorates with time. Therefore, provided the seed is stored well, in the second year you could expect around 50 per cent germination and in the third as little as 30 per cent. Before you sow, take sufficient seed out of the foil packet for the sowing and seal it immediately, place it in an airtight container, such as an old lunchbox, and keep it somewhere cool, such as the crisper drawer in a refrigerator. The best way to buy and use seed is to club together with friends and neighbours so that you can share the seed in a single packet and buy fresh each season. Of course, packets of larger seed and new cultivars will contain fewer seeds.

Don't sow all your seed at once. The seedlings will all need pricking out and potting on at the same time (both of which take a lot longer than sowing) and will require more space to grow at the same time – putting pressure on your possibly over-stretched bench and shelving space. You would be far better off sowing in small batches over a few weeks. This method gives you much greater flexibility too, so you can respond more effectively to sowing successes and failures by subsequently sowing more or less seed as required. If you have a lot of seed to deal with or have had problems sowing at the right time in the past, consider making yourself a seed organizer out of a card-index box, or similar, divided up into weeks throughout spring and summer. Then, slot each packet of seed into the week you plan to start sowing it. Seed that you intend to sow in succession can be moved on to the next sowing date after you have made the first sowing of that particular type.

If you end up with too many seedlings, it is wiser to give them away rather than growing them on yourself because they will take up valuable space and cost extra in pots and compost (soil mix). After germinating the seed you should pick the strongest seedlings for

Place the seedlings in a coldframe a week or two before planting-out time. Close the top at night and on cold days, otherwise ventilate freely. If frost threatens, cover the frame with insulation material or take the plants into a greenhouse or indoors again.

For a bumper crop from midsummer, sow runner beans in containers now, ready for planting out after the threat of frost has passed.

pricking out, because they will perform better in the long run. However, if you have sown a mixture, prick out a range of sizes, or you may select only the most vigorous cultivar from the mixture.

Hardening off

All plants raised indoors or in a greenhouse need hardening off before planting out. If this is done properly the plants will remain sturdy and healthy, but losses could be high if you move tender plants straight out into cold biting winds or hot, dry conditions outdoors after a cosseted life on the windowsill or in the greenhouse. Plants that you buy from shops and garden centres should have been hardened off before you buy them.

In the vegetable garden coldframes are frequently used to afford warmth and protection to trays of seedlings before being planted out. Aluminium coldframes have the advantage that they are light enough to move around, but they are not so good at

retaining heat. Wooden or brick-walled coldframes provide much better protection. Lights (lids) that are glazed with glass are generally preferable, but plastic can be used where there is danger of accidents – if children are likely to be in the garden, for example.

If you don't have a coldframe, you can cover plants with cloches. Alternatively, group the seed trays together in a sheltered spot outside and cover them with garden fleece or a perforated plastic floating cloche.

If you don't have a coldframe, you can cover groups of plants with cloches. Ventilate them whenever possible so that the plants become acclimatized to the cooler temperature while they are still receiving protection from the worst winds and cold.

Successional sowing and intercropping

The biggest challenge when growing your own vegetables is to have them mature at the right time so that you do not have any more gaps or gluts than necessary. Planning is of critical importance: choosing the right combination of crops and varieties, and making repeat sowings when appropriate, should enable you to approach the ideal of providing fresh produce for the kitchen daily.

Maintaining the supply

With some crops, such as peas, Brussels sprouts and cabbages, you can combine cultivars that differ in the time they take to mature. That way you can get a longer period of harvest. Of course, there may be times when you do not want to spread the harvest period. You may, for example, want to freeze a large batch of one type of vegetable for winter use.

Successional sowing

Some crops, such as lettuce, peas, spring onions (scallions), early carrots and radishes, need to be sown several times during the season to ensure a succession for the kitchen table. This is known as successional sowing. Sow these crops in short rows at regular intervals throughout the growing season. Wait until the previous sowing has germinated and started to grow before you make your next sowing.

Intercropping

If space is limited in your garden, you can make additional sowings of quick-growing crops, such as lettuce and radish, between the widely spaced rows of slower-growing types, such as Brussels sprouts and cauliflowers. This is known as intercropping. The quick-growing crops will take advantage of the space between the brassica seedlings and help to suppress weed growth too. The quick-growing crop is harvested before the brassicas need the space to grow to their full sizes.

You can use a similar technique on ground destined for late-sown or planted crops or after early-harvested crops to make the most efficient use of the growing space. And if you are really cunning you can do both. For example, a succession of lettuce crops can be sown and grown on the patch of ground planned to take a later-sown crop of corn. The earliest lettuce harvested will make room for the new corn plants and the later-cropped lettuce will mature between the corn seedlings as they grow. Another trick to try is to sow a few pots of quick-growing crops each time you sow. Grow these on in a coldframe so that they can be planted out to fill any gaps that appear as the result of losses or early harvesting.

Saving space

You can also save space by growing crops closer together than normally recommended. Root crops such as swede (rutabaga), parsnip and beetroot (beets) can be grown in this way, as can leeks, onions and many types of brassica. For example, you can grow mini-cauliflowers from summer cultivars sown in spring or early summer that are grown at much closer spacing than normal. Sow

SOWING CORN

1 Sow only when there is no risk of frost and the soil temperature has reached 10°C (50°F). In cold areas, warm up the soil with fleece or cloches for a week or two first. Alternatively, sow in pots and plant out later.

2 Sow the seeds 2.5cm (1in) deep and 8cm (3in) apart, and thin plantlets to the final recommended spacing later – typically 30cm (12in) apart each way. Sow in blocks rather than in single rows.

3 Cover with a fine net floating cloche or garden fleece. This can be left on after germination until the plants have pushed the cover up to its limit without damaging them.

4 In areas where outdoor sowing is unreliable, raise the plants in modules or peat pots. Plant them out when there is no danger of frost and after careful hardening off.

several seeds every 15cm (6in) where they are to grow, and thin these to one seedling if more than one germinates. The heads are much smaller than normal, but total yields can still be good. Thinning is a tedious but essential task. The final spacing between plants will determine both the size of the individual vegetables and the total yield. Exact spacing will often depend on whether you are more interested in the total crop or large, well-shaped individual specimens.

Multiple sowing

Some gardeners grow certain vegetables – such as carrots, beetroot, onions and leeks – in small clusters. Four to six seeds are usually sown in each cell of modular trays and planted out without any attempt to separate them. These are not normally thinned. The vegetables are usually smaller and less well shaped than those sown in rows and thinned normally, but the overall weight of crop may be good if the spacing recommended for this type of cultivation is followed.

Sow or plant corn in blocks rather than in rows to ensure a good set, because the plants are wind-pollinated, and not insect-pollinated like most other vegetables.

THINNING SEEDLINGS

1 Follow the spacing advice given on the seed packet when sowing. The packet should also recommend the ideal final spacing between plants after thinning so that all the plants left have room to grow to their optimum size.

2 Thin in stages, pulling up surplus plants between finger and thumb. The first thinning should leave the young plants twice as close as their final recommended spacing, to allow for losses after thinning.

3 Before the plants begin to compete with each other for moisture and nutrients, thin once more to the final spacing. With some crops, the thinnings can be used in the kitchen to add to salads.

Planting tender crops

Tender crops, such as tomatoes, aubergines (eggplants), marrows (large zucchini) and courgettes (zucchini), can be planted out as soon as threat of frost has passed. In milder regions, this can be around mid-spring, but in colder areas you might have to wait until late spring or even early summer before you can plant tender crops outside. Be prepared to protect vulnerable crops with a cloche or floating mulch if a late frost is forecast.

Growing beans

In mild areas runner and climbing French beans can be sown direct outside at this time of year, but in colder areas you'll have to wait until early summer or start the seeds off indoors. Canes and nets are the main methods of supporting runner and pole beans. If you use a net, choose a large-mesh net sold as a pea and bean net, and stretch it taut between well-secured posts. If you use canes, the most popular methods to use are wigwams and crossed canes. Proprietary supports are also available but, although usually very effective, they can be expensive.

Plant out tender marrows during late spring for a bumper crop of fruit that will start from midsummer and go on until autumn.

Growing tomatoes

Tomatoes are perhaps the most popular of all tender vegetables, partly because they are easy to grow, but also because they have a flavour that cannot be equalled by the commercially grown crops sold by supermarkets. They can be grown in a greenhouse or outside in all but the coldest districts where the summer is not reliably long enough for the fruit to ripen. You'll get the biggest yields from greenhouse-grown crops, while those grown outside are often tastier, especially after a long, hot summer. It is important to

PLANTING OUTDOOR TOMATOES

1 Plant at the spacing recommended for the cultivar – some grow tall and large, others remain small and compact. Always make sure they have been well hardened off.

2 In cold areas, cover plants with cloches for a few weeks, or use garden fleece to protect them on cool nights. Remove the protection on hot days.

3 Once the fleece or protection has been removed, stake the plants immediately, tying them loosely to the cane with soft string. Some dwarf varieties may not require staking.

Planting out marrows and courgettes

This marrow seedling has been raised in a degradable fibre pot. This means that it will suffer less root disturbance when planted out.

choose the right cultivar: outdoors go for 'Golden Sunrise', 'Ida Gold', 'Incas', 'Marmande Super', 'Outdoor Girl', 'Red Alert', 'Sweet 100', 'Tornado', 'Totem' or 'Tumbler'; indoors opt for 'Gemini', 'Sioux' or 'Shirley'. 'Ailsa Craig', 'Alicante', 'Gardener's Delight', 'Mirabelle', 'Sungold' and 'Tigerella' can be grown indoors or out. A few varieties, notably 'Tumbler', have been bred specifically for hanging baskets – these can produce good crops and look very attractive, but they will need frequent watering.

Tomatoes sown in late winter or early spring will have been pricked out and potted up individually into 9cm (3½in) pots. When they are 20–25cm (8–10in) tall and have their first truss of flowers starting to show colour, they are ready to plant out, provided the temperature is at least 13°C (55°F). If you haven't sown your seed yet, there is still time to do so now for a crop in late

summer. Alternatively, you can buy a limited selection of named varieties as plants from garden centres. This can be an economical way of obtaining a few plants because tomato seed is expensive and you will avoid the risks and costs involved with early sowings.

The most popular way to grow tomatoes – indoors or out – is in a growing bag. Provided you keep them well fed and watered throughout the growing season, you're more or less guaranteed a good crop. Growing bags are a cheap way to buy compost (soil mix), and because it is sterilized there will be no problems from soil-borne diseases. Pests still need to be controlled, however, otherwise quality and yields will be reduced. Staking can be a problem if you want to grow tomatoes in growing bags on a hard base. There are many proprietary designs of cane supports intended for crops such as tomatoes in growing bags, and most should last for several years. If the growing bag is positioned on soil you can push the cane through the bag into

PLANTING RUNNER AND POLE BEANS

1 Sow two seeds 5cm (2in) deep by each cane or support. Thin to one plant later if both germinate. Wait until the soil temperature is at least 12°C (54°F) before sowing. Use a soil thermometer to check.

Growing your own courgettes means you can also enjoy the flowers, which are delicious raw, steamed or fried.

the soil. Prepare the growing bag before planting by plumping it up like a pillow to loosen the growing medium. If it is to be used in a greenhouse, place it inside at least a week before planting to allow time for the compost to warm up.

2 If you raise the plants in pots, plant them out once there is no reasonable risk of frost. Use a trowel and plant them just to one side of the cane. Tie them to the cane as soon as they are tall enough and continue to tie them in.

Harvesting early crops

The earliest crops will soon be ready for harvest. Early sowings of lettuce and other leafy crops, radish, spring onions (scallions), early peas and carrots will all be reaching maturity. The last of the overwintered crops, including brassicas, leeks and root crops, will also be available for use in the kitchen. Early crops can be picked regularly as they become ready, and eaten deliciously fresh.

Young vegetables

Start pulling early carrots and radish as soon as you can see the roots are starting to swell. Early carrots take about two months from sowing to harvest. Pull them selectively, aiming to remove them when the roots are 1–1.5cm (½–⅔in) across. Thinnings of carrots can also be used in salads. Spring onions can be pulled, but do so before the bulb starts to swell. Water these crops the day before harvesting to make pulling easier.

Spinach and loose-leaf lettuce can be picked as soon as the leaves are large enough; select the largest individual leaves from each plant. Later you can cut whole plants of

STAKING AND PINCHING OUT BROAD (FAVA) BEANS

1 Pinching out the tops of the beans is good practice because it discourages blackfly. The tops can then be boiled and eaten.

2 Tall forms of broad bean will need supporting with string tied to canes that are set at intervals along the rows.

loose-leaf lettuce to leave a 2.5cm (1in) stump, which should regrow for a second crop a month or so later. Harvest cut-and-come-again lettuce as seedlings about a month after sowing. Rocket (arugula) and endive can also be harvested in less than two months after sowing. Stagger the cropping to ensure a continuous supply. With early peas, pick the pods as soon as they start to swell and before they are too large and tough. Pick them regularly thereafter to maximize the yield.

Early potatoes

Although the first crop of potatoes will not be available for a few weeks, make sure the developing tubers do not get exposed to light using a technique called earthing (hilling) up (see right). If they are exposed, their skins will turn green and the tubers will be poisonous to eat. By drawing soil into a ridge over the potatoes you will help cover any that are near to the surface and keep weeds under control as you go. Do this regularly until the foliage of adjacent rows touches. Earthing up also encourages formation of new tubers from the newly-covered stems.

You can, however, get new potatoes available for harvest at any time of the year by growing them in large containers. A large plastic wheelie bin (wheeled trash can) is ideal, since it is about the right size and is easy to move around. First drill drainage holes in the base, then half-fill with a 50:50 mix of good garden soil and old potting compost (soil mix) – a useful way of recycling the compost from last year's hanging baskets and patio containers. Mix in a slow-release fertilizer to feed the crop

HARVESTING EARLY CROPS

1 Radishes are harvested simply by pulling them from the ground by hand. They should be harvested when they are large enough to eat. Do not let them get large and woody.

2 Spring onions (scallions) can be harvested by pulling them from the ground by hand, but you may need to loosen the soil gently with a fork as you pull.

throughout its life. Chit the tubers before planting, which means leaving them in a light, frost-free place, such as on a windowsill, until sprouts grow to about 2cm (¾in) long. Plant them in a large pot, and when they are well-established plants with 20cm (8in) of topgrowth, plant them into the half-filled bin. Gradually add more compost as the shoots grow (without covering the leaves) until the bin is full. Keep frost-free at all times. Seed potatoes planted in early summer will be ready for harvest in late autumn, those planted in late winter can be harvested by mid-spring, and a crop planted in early spring will be ready by midsummer. Carefully push your hand into the compost to search and remove any chicken-egg-sized tubers. Lightly firm the soil mix after harvesting and leave the plants to grow on for a couple of weeks before probing again. Alternatively, you can harvest all the tubers in one go by emptying the bin completely. This is a particularly worthwhile method of growing new potatoes for the Christmas table.

Radishes are extremely fast-growing. When harvesting, discard any that have become large or old, as they will be too woody and hot to eat.

PROTECTING AND EARTHING (HILLING) UP POTATOES

1 Potatoes will usually recover from slight frost damage, but if you know that a frost is forecast once the shoots are through the ground, cover the plants with newspaper or garden fleece. Remove the cover the next morning once the frost has gone.

2 Start earthing up the potatoes when the shoots are about 15cm (6in) high. Use a draw hoe to pull up the soil either side of the row. Do this carefully so that you do not damage the stems with the hoe, which will leave the plants susceptible to pests and diseases.

3 Continue to earth up in stages, as the potatoes grow, until the soil creates a mound about 15cm (6in) high. Regular earthing up not only prevents light from reaching the tubers but also prevents weed seedlings from getting established.

Herbs in containers

Many herbs make ideal container plants. Not only is this a convenient way of growing them, but there are a number of advantages compared to growing them in the garden border. Most herbs are native to the Mediterranean area and so like the well-drained conditions a container offers. Indeed, if your soil is too heavy to grow herbs, you can still grow these plants successfully in pots on the patio.

A movable feast

Herbs in containers are easy to move around so that you can bring them near to the kitchen door when they are in season and hide them away somewhere less prominent at other times of the year. In addition, when you go away, you can move the containers to a shady spot to reduce the need for watering.

If you are mixing herbs in a larger container, group those with similar requirements to make looking after them easier. Short-lived herbs and those used in large amounts, such as basil and chives, are worth growing in separate pots so that they are easily replaced when they are over or all used up. Vigorous herbs, such as mint, which send spreading and penetrating shoots beneath the soil's surface, can be kept under control by being grown in a pot (see opposite). Mints don't like to dry out, so sink the pot nearly rim-deep into a larger container or the ground, or grow them in a glazed pot placed in semi-shade.

The main disadvantage of growing herbs in containers is that they will need watering regularly throughout the growing season. Perennial herbs will also need watering during dry spells at other times of the year, and tender varieties will be more susceptible to frost than those planted in the ground.

Choosing a container

Choose a large container for perennial herbs and medium-sized pots – at least 20cm (8in) diameter

PLANTING UP A HERB POT

1 An ornamental herb pot is best filled in stages. Cover the drainage hole with crocks before adding free-draining compost (soil mix) to the height of the first planting pockets.

2 Using small plants, knock them out of their pots and push the rootballs through the holes in the planting pockets. Reduce the size of the rootball if necessary.

3 Add more of the compost and repeat with the next row of planting holes. Unless the pot is very large, don't try to pack many herbs into the top because there will be too much competition. A single well-grown plant often looks much better.

4 Large earthenware pots can look just as good as herb pots with planting pockets if you plant them imaginatively. If you have a half-barrel use this instead. Place a bold shrubby herb, such as sweet bay (*Laurus nobilis*), in the centre.

5 Until the sweet bay grows to fill the pot, you should be able to fit a collection of smaller herbs around the edge. Avoid mints, however, which are usually too rampant to use with other plants and will quickly outgrow their allotted space.

CONTROLLING MINTS

1 A growing bag is an ideal home for mints. They will be happy for a couple of seasons, and then are easily removed and replanted for a fresh start. Choose small, healthy plants that will establish quickly.

2 Instead of filling the growing bag with one kind of mint, try planting a collection of perhaps four to six different kinds. There are a surprising number of different mints, and the flavours vary quite widely.

3 If you want to plant your mint in the border (which will avoid the chore of watering it frequently), plant it in an old bucket or a large pot. It is important to make sure that there are drainage holes in the bottom, and fill with soil or compost (soil mix) before you plant the mint.

4 Mint spreads quickly, and to prevent its roots growing into the surrounding soil, you should make sure that the rim of the pot is just visible above the surface. Lift, divide and replant annually or every second spring, to maintain vigour. Take a piece of root from the old plant.

Choosing herbs

Hanging baskets	Large containers
Basil	Bay
Marjoram	Hyssop
Rosemary	Lemon verbena
(prostrate)	Rosemary
Sage	Sage
Thyme	
Winter savory	*Growing bags*
	Basil
Small containers	Lemon balm
Basil	Mint
Chamomile	Parsley
Marjoram	Sorrel
Mint	
Summer savory	
Thyme	
Winter savory	

After planting, position Mediterranean herbs in a sunny spot on the patio. Many, including thyme, rosemary, lavender and marjoram, will be most aromatic and flavoursome when grown in full sun, and in poor soil – feeding increases growth, but the flavour will be less intense.

– for the rest. This will make watering less onerous. Porous terracotta is ideal for drought-tolerant Mediterranean herbs, but moisture-loving herbs, such as dill, fennel, lovage and coriander (cilantro), will do better in a glazed or plastic pot. If you choose an ornamental herb pot, like the one right, it is best treated as a short-term home to be replanted annually. Bear in mind that the tapered shape will make it difficult to remove well-established plants. For the best effect, you can create a theme of matching styles or colours, so that the container display looks co-ordinated. A loam-based compost (soil mix) such as John Innes No. 2 usually gives the best results, though an all-purpose compost can also be used.

You can grow herbs in all sorts of containers, from hanging baskets, in which smaller perennial herbs such as golden marjoram and thyme work well, to growing bags, which could accommodate a thriving crop of basil. In a windowbox outside the kitchen window try growing herbs in individual containers that can be easily slotted in and out as they come into season. Larger containers, such as half-barrels, are ideal for shrubby herbs, such as bay and rosemary.

Ornamental herb pots make wonderful garden features. Here, a selection of cascading thymes are used to good effect.

Climate control

It is essential to keep control of the greenhouse environment if you are to achieve the best possible results from greenhouse crops. At this time of the year, temperatures can rocket as soon as the sun comes out, causing plants considerable stress. Ideally, aim to maintain a temperature of 21–26°C (70–79°F) for most plants through the careful use of ventilation, shading and damping down.

Using ventilation

At this time of year, you should be able to control temperatures sufficiently by opening vents in the greenhouse on warm days and closing them again at night. By opening a vent along the ridge of the greenhouse and one at the side,

you'll create a 'chimney effect' as the hot, humid air escapes through the roof, drawing in cooler, drier air through the side. You can make the whole job easier by installing automatic vent-openers that will respond to the prevailing conditions. There are devices designed to open both hinged and louvred vents. Look for models that are spring-loaded so you can close the vent tightly during the night. For adequate ventilation on warm days you will need several opening vents in the roof and along the sides of the greenhouse. Ideally, they should be equal to about one-fifth of the floor area of your greenhouse. Most greenhouses are supplied with far fewer vents, so it is worth considering installing extra roof and side vents from the outset.

Providing shading

When the weather warms up in the early summer, opening vents alone will not be sufficient to keep the greenhouse cool. You will need to take steps to reduce the amount of sunlight that enters the greenhouse by applying shading washes to the glass or installing blinds or shading fabric. Washes that are applied to the glass are the cheapest and easiest option, and one application alone will last for the whole of the season. The wash does not vary the amount of shade it provides in response to changing weather conditions, so it can reduce crop growth in bad years. However, there is one type, called Varishade, that turns transparent when it gets wet, which means that more light can get through in rainy

You can keep temperatures inside a greenhouse under control from late spring onwards through careful ventilation, shading and damping down. You can also position sun-loving plants such as tomatoes so that they provide shade for other plants.

If you are not at home during the hottest part of the day, automatic vent-openers which respond to temperature can be a great help in regulating the atmosphere inside the greenhouse.

Moving plants outdoors

Container-grown tender and semi-tender shrubs and climbers, such as citrus trees, which have been protected in the greenhouse over the winter months, can be placed outside in a sheltered spot once the threat of frost has passed. Don't forget to keep them well watered and feed them regularly unless you have applied a slow-release fertilizer that will provide sufficient nutrients for the whole season. Protect them on cool nights if necessary.

weather, and then clouds over again when it dries. If you decide to have blinds or fabric to provide shade, then they are best fitted to the outside of the greenhouse where they will most effectively prevent the sun's heat getting through the glass. If they are fitted inside, some of the heat from the sun will penetrate the glass, warming the air inside the greenhouse.

Staying cool

During the hottest weather of the summer even these precautions may not be enough, especially if the weather is still. You can improve ventilation further by installing an electric fan that will move air in and out of the greenhouse. There are solar-powered devices available so you don't need to worry about wiring it into the mains. Damping

down is another option. This involves wetting the floor and staging inside the greenhouse on hot days, so that energy is absorbed as the water evaporates and is carried out of the greenhouse in the form of water vapour. Some greenhouse plants are better adapted than others to the scorching effects of the sun, so you can arrange the greenhouse so that sun-loving crops, such as tomatoes, are grown on the sunniest side and provide shade for more sun-sensitive crops.

KEEPING YOUR GREENHOUSE COOL

1 It is vital not to let greenhouses overheat. A maximum/minimum thermometer is an invaluable piece of equipment, not only showing the current temperature but recording the highest that has been reached during the day, as well as the coolest at night.

2 You need to reduce the amount of sun entering the greenhouse during the hottest part of the year. Shading, in the form of temporary netting, helps to keep the temperature down and also protects the plants from the scorching effects of the sun.

3 Splashing or spraying water over the greenhouse floor helps to create a humid atmosphere and reduce greenhouse temperatures: energy is absorbed as the water evaporates. This traditional technique is known as damping down.

Training crops

Greenhouse crops always used to be grown in the greenhouse border, and the soil changed periodically. This was considered risky, and ring culture became fashionable. In more recent times growing bags have been in favour. All three systems have merits and drawbacks, so you can choose whichever appeals to you most or seems the easiest.

Planting methods

Growing crops in the border soil is the best option if you find regular watering a chore. Because the plants' roots are able to tap into water reserves deep in the ground, they will need less frequent watering. The soil will need to be improved by applying well-rotted organic matter and a general fertilizer before planting. If yields drop after a few years, there may have been a build-up of soil-borne pests and diseases and so you will need to remove the soil and replace with fresh from the garden.

Growing bags contain sterilized compost (soil mix) and so there is no problem with soil-borne pests. You will get very good results provided you can keep the crops well fed and watered. This may mean watering them several times a day in the hot weather, but you can get automatic watering devices that will make the job much easier. Feed fruiting crops with a high-potash liquid feed, such as that sold for tomatoes, every two weeks, once the fruit has started to develop.

Training tomatoes

Plant stocky plants in spring when the first flower truss is starting to show colour. Throw away any very

GROWING METHODS FOR TOMATOES

1 Always dig in as much well-rotted manure or garden compost as you can spare and rake in a general garden fertilizer before you plant your tomatoes. Although they can be planted earlier, most gardeners find late spring is a good time because the greenhouse usually has more space once the bedding plants have been planted out in the garden.

2 Most greenhouse varieties grow tall and need support. Tall canes are a convenient method if you have just a few plants, but if you have a lot of plants the string method may be more suitable. Tie lengths of string vertically to horizontal wires adjacent to the plants and use these to support the main stem as it grows.

3 With ring culture, the water-absorbing roots grow into a moist aggregate and the feeding roots into special bottomless pots filled with potting compost (soil mix). Take out a trench about 15–23cm (6–9in) deep in the greenhouse border and line it with a waterproof plastic (this minimizes soil-borne disease contamination).

4 Fill the trench with fine gravel, coarse grit or expanded clay granules. Then place the special bottomless ring culture pots on the aggregate base and fill them with a good potting compost. Firm the compost lightly to remove air pockets.

5 Plant into the ring and insert a cane or provide an alternative support. Water only into the ring at first. Once the plant is established and some roots have penetrated into the aggregate, water only the aggregate and feed through the pot.

6 Growing bags are less trouble than ring culture to set up, but you still have to feed plants regularly, and watering can be more difficult to control unless you use an automatic system. Insert a cane through the bag or use a string support.

SUPPORTING TOMATOES

Tie vertical strings between horizontal wires alongside each plant and use these to provide support for the growing main stem.

spindly plants or those with yellowing foliage because they will never recover fully. String is a simple and economical way to support your tomatoes. Fix one wire as high as practicable from one end of the greenhouse to the other, aligning it above the border, and another one just above the ground. Tie lengths of string between the wires, in line with each plant. You don't need to tie the plant to its support – just loop the string around the growing tip so that it forms a spiral.

Training cucumbers

Cucumbers are also best grown as cordons, with a single main stem tied to a vertical cane or string. Try growing cucumbers in growing bags on the greenhouse staging. Insert canes between the growing bags and the eaves, and fix horizontal wires along the length of the roof. You can then train the growth along the roof and the cucumbers will hang down. A standard growing bag should hold about two cucumber plants. Do not overcrowd the plants. Tie the plant in to the support as it grows and pinch out any sideshoots, flowers and tendrils until it reaches the first wire. Then train two sideshoots along each horizontal wire, removing sideshoots only.

Many modern cucumber varieties produce only female flowers, but some greenhouse varieties produce both male and female blooms (the female bloom has a small swelling at its base). Pinch out the male flowers before they pollinate the female ones, because the resulting cucumbers will taste bitter.

Growing peppers

Sweet peppers (*Capsicum*) like the same conditions as tomatoes and so are easy to grow alongside them. Pinch out the tips of the young plants after planting to encourage sideshoots to grow. Provide a single cane support for each plant and tie all the stems loosely to it. Keep the compost moist and mist plants to discourage red spider mite.

Tender sweet peppers are easy to grow in the border soil or, as here, in growing bags supported with canes. They change from green to red or yellow as they ripen, so pick them when they are at the stage you want.

Summer

Although most of the hard work has been completed in the spring rush, the garden is still a hive of activity during early summer. The bulk of the sowing and pricking out will be complete, so the challenge is to keep your new plants growing strongly, making sure they don't go short of water and protecting them from pests and diseases. This is the ideal time to prune fruit trees and bushes, and weeds will need to be kept under control. With the threat of frost past in all but the coldest regions, it is a time to enjoy the fruits of your labours. Early crops, such as beetroot (beets), broad (fava) beans, cabbage, carrots, early potatoes, carrots and peas, are ready to eat, as are perennial crops such as globe artichokes, asparagus and rhubarb. As summer progresses French (green) and runner beans, courgettes (zucchini), onions and lettuces will be ready for use, along with sun-loving crops such as tomatoes, corn and (bell) peppers. Many fruit crops will also be ready for harvest from midsummer onwards.

The first of the apples will be ready to pick in late summer. Harvest them over several weeks, as they reach the right stage of maturity.

Watering the vegetable plot

Making sure that your crops don't run short of water is one of the most important aspects of successful vegetable gardening. A dry spell will cause the plant to suffer a check in growth and subsequent yields will be reduced. How much water you should apply will depend on where you live, on the soil in your garden and, above all, on the prevailing weather conditions.

How much to water?

Judging how much water is required is made more complicated because not all vegetables require the same amount. When you should apply it also depends on the crop you are growing. From a watering perspective, vegetables can be split into three main groups: those that benefit from watering during any dry spell to ensure they do not go short of water; those that need watering at critical stages of development to ensure a good crop; and those that can look after themselves provided the drought isn't prolonged. This last group includes perennial crops, such as asparagus and artichokes, and other crops well adapted to coping with drought, such as carrots, beetroot (beets), parsnips, swedes (rutabagas) and turnips.

Vegetables that produce lush, fleshy growth, such as celery, lettuce, Chinese cabbage and spinach, as well as those that produce succulent tubers or fruits, such as new potatoes, tomatoes, marrows (large zucchini) and courgettes (zucchini), need watering the most. Aim to apply 20 litres per square metre (4 gallons per square yard) each week during dry spells to give maximum yields. Most beans and peas fall into the second category, along with maincrop potatoes and corn. These crops should not be allowed to go short of water during critical stages in their development. With peas and beans, apply 20 litres per square metre (4 gallons per square yard) each week as soon as the pods have set when the weather is dry. If you are growing corn, apply this amount when the tassels first appear. With maincrop potatoes, water well just the once when in flower (this is about the time the

Leafy vegetables, such as lettuce and spinach, as well as crops that produce succulent tubers or fruits, such as new potatoes and tomatoes, need thorough and regular watering.

WATERING METHODS

A good way to water a vegetable garden is with a watering can. Water can then be applied not only in the right quantity but also right to the plant's roots.

A seep or drip hose can be laid along a row of plants and will water only the immediate area. The water slowly seeps out of the pipe and soaks into the soil.

The delivery nozzle of this drip-feed watering system is held in position with a pipe peg, so that the head can deliver water to an individual plant.

tubers start to swell). Excessive watering before these critical stages can be detrimental, encouraging the crops to put on excess leafy growth at the expense of edible roots, and even delaying the harvest time.

Efficient watering

Watering can be one of the most time-consuming tasks in the vegetable garden in a dry year, so it makes sense to be as efficient as possible by applying the water exactly where it is required. One of the most common mistakes is to splash water all over the place by switching on a sprinkler, rather than concentrating it along the rows of crops. It is also a mistake to water little and often because a lot of water will be lost by evaporation and only the surface of the soil will be soaked, which encourages shallow rooting and makes the crops even more susceptible to drought.

Create ridges either side of the row or around widely spaced crops so that the water is held in the right place until it has had a chance to soak in. Sink bottomless upturned plastic drinks bottles into the ground next to thirsty plants such as

tomatoes. You can also buy watering spikes that screw on to the top of the bottles, and are then pushed into the ground. You then fill the bottle with water, and it sinks straight to the roots. The soil surface will remain dry, reducing losses due to

evaporation as well as preventing weed seeds germinating. Lay seep hose along rows of crops to cut down on watering time. Watering in the evening, rather than in the heat of the day, also helps reduce loss through evaporation.

Collect your own water

You can easily collect sufficient water in a water butt to keep a collection of acid-loving plants happy all summer long. You can also get kits to link water butts together to create a more complex garden water storage system.

Place a water butt beneath the gutter of a greenhouse, shed or garage to catch the water as it runs off the roof. Rainwater is slightly acidic so is ideal for watering acid-loving plants, especially if you live in a hard-water area. It will also conserve water and money spent on metered water. Make sure the butt is raised so that there is room to get a watering can under the tap. Keep the butt covered so that the water remains sweet and clean.

You can also recycle water that has been used for washing or bathing in the house. Known as 'grey water', this is suitable for applying to established plants in borders and on lawns, but it is best used immediately, not stored.

Saving rainwater not only reduces bills if your supply is metered, but also provides suitable supplies for acid-loving plants.

Controlling weeds

Even in a well-organized and well-maintained plot, weed control takes up to 20 per cent of the time spent tending the vegetables. You can save yourself a lot of time, therefore, by avoiding weed problems to start with and by being efficient about tackling infestations as they occur. Not only do weeds rob crops of valuable water and nutrients, but they can also attract pests and harbour a number of fungal diseases – bad news if you want to maintain healthy crops.

Ways to succeed

Thorough soil preparation during the winter and early spring is the key to success. As long as you have removed all perennial weed roots from the soil, you will only have new seedlings to deal with while the crop is growing. These can be controlled in four ways: manual weeding, mechanical weeding, mulching to prevent weeds from germinating, and chemical controls.

Because most vegetables are grown in rows, the majority of weed seedlings can be effectively controlled by hoeing (mechanical weeding). Keep your hoe sharp at all

DIGGING UP WEEDS

1 Weeding with a hand fork is often the best option when delicate plants are spaced very closely together.

2 Sowing crops in rows in a designated vegetable plot makes weeding much easier with the aid of a specialized tool.

times so that it is easier to use. Hold it so that it slices through weeds just below the surface rather than uprooting them and disturbing the soil. The best time to hoe is during the morning on a warm, dry day. The weeds can be left to wither and die on the surface so that you don't have to spend time and energy gathering them up. If you have neglected weeding for a while, first remove by hand (manual weeding) all weeds that are flowering and threatening to set seed. Also remove all perennial weeds. Do this when the

weather is dry but the soil is moist, so that the weeds can be easily pulled up complete with their roots. Then hoe off the rest of the weeds as before. You can also get a wide range of specialist tools for weeding between crops as well as mechanical devices. These are really only worth considering if you have a very large vegetable garden.

A few crops, such as corn, are easily damaged by hoeing, and they are best grown through a mulch of black plastic sheeting so that the need for weeding is eliminated. You

DEALING WITH WEEDS

1 Perennial weeds that have long, penetrating roots are best forked up. Loosen the roots with a fork and hold the stem close to its base as you pull up the whole plant. If you don't get all the root out, the remaining piece will probably regrow.

2 Hoeing is one of the best forms of weed control, but it needs to be done regularly. Slice the weeds off just beneath the soil surface, preferably when the soil is dry. Keep beds and borders hoed, as well as the vegetable garden.

3 Contact chemical weedkillers are useful if you want to clear an area of ground quickly and easily. Some – which normally only kill the topgrowth, so are better for annuals than for problem perennial weeds – leave the area safe to replant after a day.

can also reduce the need for weeding between rows of vegetables by laying black plastic between the rows.

Widely spaced transplanted crops, such as cabbages and cauliflowers, can be planted through slits cut into a black plastic sheet mulch laid over the vegetable plot. Prepare the soil well before laying the plastic, removing all perennial weeds. You can sink saucers of beer or milk under slits in the plastic, to trap slugs, as these are likely to congregate under the plastic. Bury the edges of the plastic in slit trenches made with a spade down either side and at both ends of the plot. Then cut cross-shaped slits at the correct planting distance and plant as normal. You can also grow maincrop potatoes in this way. In this instance, plant as normal and cover the surface of the soil with the black plastic mulch. When the shoots reach the surface and start to push the plastic from below, cut the cross-shaped slits to expose them.

Black plastic is also useful for covering the vacant ground between crops to prevent weeds becoming a problem. Cover the black plastic with a layer of soil or chipped bark

Keep weeds under control at all times if you want to maximize yields from your vegetable plot. They not only rob your soil of moisture and nutrients, but they can also harbour pests and diseases. Large, leafy plants covering most of the surface will greatly reduce weed germination.

to disguise it. Old carpet can also be used to suppress weeds and has the advantage of allowing water to percolate through and into the soil.

Although the range of weedkillers you can use on the vegetable plot is limited, they are useful around perennial crops, such as asparagus and rhubarb, to keep perennial weeds under control.

Vegetables to grow through a plastic mulch

Brussels sprout	Pepper (outdoor)
Cabbage	Potato
Cauliflower	Pumpkin
Courgette	Sweet corn
Marrow	Tomato
Melon (outdoor)	(outdoor)

4 Systemic weedkillers kill the whole plant, including the roots. If weeds are widespread, large areas of ground can be sprayed, but you can paint some formulations on to individual leaves to kill the weed without harming neighbouring plants.

5 Mulches are very effective at controlling weeds by preventing weed seeds from germinating. In the vegetable garden various forms of plastic sheeting are a cost-effective method. The sheeting has lots of tiny holes to allow moisture to penetrate to the ground.

6 Where appearance matters, such as in a combined vegetable and flower border, use an organic material such as chipped bark, garden compost or cocoa shells. If the ground is cleared of weeds first, a mulch at least 5cm (2in) thick will suppress most weeds.

Summer harvesting

By early summer many crops have reached maturity and are ready to harvest. It is important to pick each crop when it is in prime condition. Aim to harvest as quickly as possible but take care not to damage the vegetable in the process because this can encourage storage rots later. Pick vegetables that are young and tender for freezing but allow them to reach full maturity if they are destined for dry storage.

Asparagus

Established beds should be cropping from early summer for about six weeks. Stop harvesting during mid-summer. Do not start harvesting from new asparagus beds until they have been established for three years. Using a sharp knife, cut the spears 5cm (2in) below ground level when they reach about 10–15cm (4–6in) high. Use as fresh as possible after harvest or remove the lower scales and trim to length before blanching.

Beetroot (beets)

Pull roots for salads when young and tender – usually about golf-ball size. Lift maincrop beets before they become tough and inedible. Remove every other root from the row to leave the remainder to grow on for harvesting in late summer. Once the leaves begin to wilt, twist off foliage from the root to stop them bleeding.

Eat cabbages when they are fresh and crisp, when the heads are firm. Cut them off cleanly with a sharp knife. A second head sometimes grows from the stalk.

Broad (fava) beans

Harvest early, as soon as the beans start to show, so they can be used immature, like snap peas, in early summer. Later, harvest maincrop before the beans are fully formed and the stem goes woody. Eat fresh or blanch and freeze.

Cabbages

Spring and summer cabbages should be cut when heads are firm and crisp, and eaten fresh. It's sometimes possible to get a second crop by leaving a stalk about 10cm (4in) long in the ground and making an X-shaped cut in the top.

Carrots

Maincrop varieties should be available from early summer, 10 weeks after sowing. Pull selectively, aiming

HARVESTING LEAFY CROPS

1 Harvest hearting lettuces when the "heart" feels firm. Use a sharp knife to cut through the stalk.

2 Spinach is a very easy crop to harvest. When you require some, simply cut away the young leaves with a pair of sharp scissors.

to remove them when the roots are 1–1.5cm (½–⅔in) across. Thinnings of carrots can also be used in salads. On lighter soils pull carrots by hand, but on heavier ground you will need to ease them out with a fork. Refirm any that remain afterwards. Water the ground along the row the day before to make harvesting easier. Twist off the foliage immediately after harvest.

Early potatoes

Harvest when tubers are hen's egg size and the skin rubs off easily, which is usually when the flowers open on the plant. Excavate the soil alongside the row to make sure the tubers are large enough before you lift the whole plant. Eat fresh.

Globe artichokes

Established plants will be producing buds ready to be harvested by the end of early summer. Cut 5cm (2in) below the bud when the scales are still tightly closed. Once the terminal bud has been removed from each plant, new buds will be produced on sideshoots lower down for a late summer harvest. Eat fresh.

Peas

Harvest peas grown for their pods when the peas are just starting to form. Peas grown for their seeds should be harvested when pods swell and contain peas that are sweet and soft. Pick regularly to keep the plant producing new pods. Do not leave old pods on the plant, otherwise the peas will be dry and starchy and yields will drop off. Eat fresh, or shell and blanch before freezing.

Perpetual spinach

Regularly pick over spinach, removing the leaves while they are small, to maintain a continuous

HARVESTING BEETROOT

Harvest beetroot (beet) by pulling it by hand from the ground. In heavier soils a fork may be needed to loosen the roots.

HARVESTING CARROTS

Short varieties of carrot can be pulled out by hand, but longer ones and those grown on heavier soils will need digging out with a fork.

crop. Larger leaves can also be harvested but discard the tough mid-rib before you cook them. Eat fresh or freeze.

Rhubarb

Start harvesting from established plants as soon as stems are large enough. Pull individual stems by holding them near to the base and

HARVESTING ASPARAGUS

Make an oblique cut 5cm (2in) below the ground. Asparagus plants should be left to build up for three years before cropping.

HARVESTING GLOBE ARTICHOKES

Harvest a globe artichoke when the scales are tightly closed by cutting the stem just below the head.

giving a sharp twist to break them away cleanly from the crown. Do not leave any broken stems on the plant because this can allow infections to take hold in the crown. Always leave three or four mature leaves on the plant to keep it growing vigorously and remove any flowering stems as soon as you notice them. Eat fresh or freeze.

Pruning tree fruit

There are a number of advantages to be gained from pruning fruit trees in summer. Unlike winter pruning, which increases the vigour of a plant, pruning in summer tends to decrease the tree's response to being cut back. This means that this is a good time to prune if you want to keep a tree small. Pruning at this time of the year also helps to open up the canopy, so that those branches that remain will get more sunlight and the fruit they carry will be of a higher quality and will ripen earlier.

Why prune?

Neglected trees often produce their fruit out of reach, high up in the canopy, with few fruits set lower down. You can remedy this problem in summer by cutting back one or two of the main branches to a more horizontal side branch lower down. Any tree that has failed to set any fruit is more likely to put its energies into new growth, causing it to become overcrowded. If left unpruned, next year's crop is likely to consist of small, flavourless fruit that may be

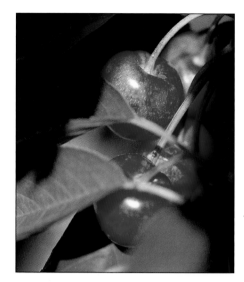

Cherries are best pruned during the summer because they are less likely to be infected by the debilitating silver leaf disease.

PRUNING FAN-SHAPED APRICOTS

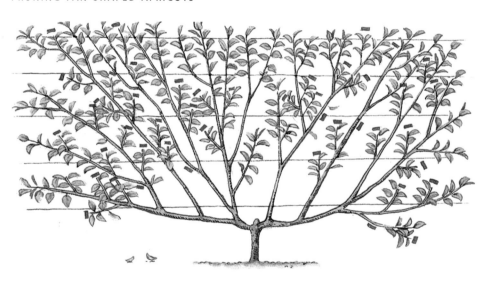

Once the fan has been established, the object of subsequent pruning is to maintain the shape. Cut out any shoots that are pointing in the wrong direction, especially those that point towards or away from the wall. Thin new shoots, leaving one every 15cm (6in). Prune the remaining shoots to five leaves in the spring and then again, after fruiting, back to three leaves.

so numerous that the tree fails to set any fruit the following year, starting the unsatisfactory cycle known as biennial bearing. The best way to deal with this sort of overcrowded growth is to remove all dead or damaged branches as well as any that are crossing or growing strongly vertically. Retain the most widely spaced and most horizontal-growing branches.

Summer pruning should only be carried out on well-established trees that have put on all their extension growth for the current year, otherwise pruning will encourage a thicket of sideshoots. If the base of the new shoot has started to turn brown and woody, the shoot will have stopped growing and is starting to mature. The growth should be stiff and not whippy when pulled downwards by the tip.

Plums and cherries

These trees, which are prone to a debilitating disease called silver leaf, are less likely to be infected when pruned in summer because there are fewer disease spores around then and the pruning cuts should heal more quickly when the tree is in vigorous

PRUNING FAN-SHAPED CHERRIES

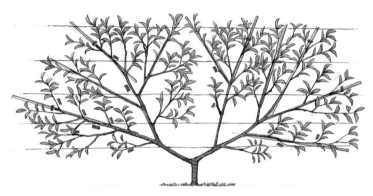

To maintain the shape, remove any shoots that are pointing in the wrong direction. To ensure that there is a constant supply of new wood, cut back in summer all shoots that have fruited, as far back as the next new shoot. Tie these new shoots to the cane and wire framework.

PRUNING FAN-SHAPED PLUMS

Remove all new shoots that face towards or away from the wall. Then cut back all new shoots to about six leaves, leaving any that are needed to fill in gaps in the framework. In autumn, after cropping, further cut back the shoots to three leaves.

growth. Cherries are also prone to bacterial canker diseases which can be largely avoided by pruning in summer. It is not a good idea to prune heavily unless absolutely necessary. Once the initial shape is determined, most well-established trees do not need pruning apart from the removal of dead or damaged stems or branches. Simply prune to keep the canopy open and to maintain good health. Remove the dead or damaged branches first and thin the remaining ones as necessary.

However, it may be worth taking a risk with old, neglected cherries that fail to produce a decent crop by pruning heavily in summer. Prune back one in three of the oldest branches to a side branch lower down. New, vigorous and productive shoots may well grow in the years to come.

If suckers are growing around the base, remove these by pulling them off rather than cutting with secateurs (pruners) because pruning them will encourage new suckers to sprout.

Apricots

Most apricots are produced on the old wood, so little pruning is required other than to remove exhausted old wood every few years to maintain vigour and fruiting potential. Trees trained as fans should be pruned in summer by removing any laterals that are growing towards or away from the wall or fence and by cutting back the laterals that remain to 8cm (3in). Any new laterals produced as the summer progresses should be removed during late summer.

Once the framework of a damson tree has been established, little pruning should be necessary apart from the removal of dead or damaged wood.

Codling moth traps

Apples and sometimes pears may be attacked by codling moths, which lay eggs on young fruitlets. The grubs feed on the flesh, causing the fruit to ripen and fall early. The flesh if tunnelled is full of excreta ('frass'). You can control codling moths to some extent by tying corrugated cardboard around the trunk in autumn to lure overwintering caterpillars. Destroy any that are found. You can also control the adults by using a pheromone trap that attracts the male moths, preventing them from mating with the females. One trap per five trees should be sufficient.

Pruning and propagating soft fruit

Summer is a good time to prune soft fruit, such as gooseberries and red and white currants, as well as raspberries, because you can combine harvesting with the pruning process. You need to prune trained forms of these bushes in summer to keep them in shape. Overcrowded and unproductive bushes can also be pruned now by removing one stem in three, taking out the oldest stems first. After three years all the old wood will have been replaced with new, vigorous and productive stems.

Pruning bushes

Gooseberries and red and white currants can be pruned in summer by cutting back all sideshoots to five leaves of this year's growth. The main leader of each bush is not normally pruned at this time of year unless it is diseased. For example, gooseberries, and sometimes currants, that have been attacked by gooseberry mildew can benefit from the tipping back of new growth. The disease starts as a white, powdery deposit on the shoot tips and youngest leaves but progresses to attack fruit, eventually distorting new growth. Opening up the bush and improving airflow, as well as

Check ripening strawberries every day and pick the fruits when they are red all over. Eat fresh straight away or keep them somewhere cool for a few days.

removing infected shoots, will help to control the disease. However, you will have to spray with a systemic fungicide as soon as symptoms are seen for effective control.

Pruning cordons

All the sideshoots on plants trained on a single main stem should be cut back to four leaves. If the cordon has grown beyond the top of its support, cut back the top shoot to a plump bud at the desired height. Alternatively, pinch out these shoots to the desired length when they have put on about 15cm (6in) of growth. Any suckers should be removed by pulling them out rather than trimming with secateurs (pruners).

Pruning after harvest

Blackcurrants, blackberries and raspberries can be pruned straight after harvesting is complete, or you can wait until autumn. The old, fruiting canes of blackberries and

raspberries should be cut down to ground level. Tie in new canes to their supports. Blackcurrant stems that have borne fruit should be cut out. Alternatively, combine the harvesting and pruning process to help save time and energy, by cutting out the fruit-laden branches of blackcurrants. These can then be

GROWING STRAWBERRIES

Place a layer of straw under the leaves of the strawberry plants in order to prevent the developing fruit from getting muddy or covered with dirt.

PRUNING BLACKCURRANTS

After planting, cut blackcurrant bushes back to a single bud above ground. The following winter, remove any weak or misplaced growth. Subsequent pruning should take place after fruiting and consists of cutting out up to a third of two-year-old or older wood in order to stimulate new growth.

LAYERING BLACKBERRIES

1 Choose a healthy shoot, then dig a hole near the tip and bend down the tip to bury it in the soil.

2 After a short period the tip will have produced roots. It can then be cut from the parent plant and replanted where required.

3 If you would like to have potted specimens, bury a flowerpot in the ground, fill it with compost (soil mix) and bury the tip in this.

taken to the kitchen where they can be stripped of fruit more easily and the spent stems discarded.

Propagate soft fruit

Strawberries produce their best crop during the second and third years after planting. Thereafter, the yields will drop off as the health of the crop deteriorates. For this reason it is a good idea to replace the whole crop every three or four years with

Once blackberry canes have fruited in autumn, cut them back to ground level and tie in new ones to replace those that have been cut out.

new plants. The cheapest way to do this is to raise your own plants by rooting runners from healthy, heavily cropping plants.

Strawberries can be propagated at this time of year by rooting runners. Simply sink a series of 9cm (3½in) pots full of fresh potting compost (soil mix) into the ground around the parent plant. Water the compost well, then select four or five strong, healthy runners and peg one plantlet down into each pot of compost using a piece of bent wire so that the base of the plantlet is in good contact with the moist compost. After a month or so, the plantlet will have rooted well and can be severed from the parent plant.

Blackberries and hybrid berries, such as tayberries, can be increased by layering. With these plants the tip of the shoot is pegged down in contact with the soil or compost in a pot. Dig a hole about 15cm (6in) deep and bury the shoot tip by replacing the soil. After the shoot tip has rooted, sever it from the parent plant, leaving 30cm (12in) of the original cane.

Raspberries naturally produce suckers alongside an established row and these can be removed once well

rooted by severing the stem from the main parent plant and replanting the rooting sucker as new stock if it is required. Red, white and blackcurrants are easy to propagate from hardwood cuttings in winter.

Cut back strawberries

Once the crop has been harvested, cut off all the old leaves back to the main crown and dispose of them or burn them. Do not compost them or leave them lying around the garden as they will help carry over pests and diseases to next year's crop. Runners should also be removed, unless you are using them to propagate new plants. If you used a straw mulch, you should remove this at the same time and destroy it.

Watering and feeding greenhouse crops

Watering is a year-round task in the greenhouse, but the summer months are the most demanding. Plants growing in containers, such as pots and growing bags, are entirely dependent on you for their food and water, and this may mean watering more than once a day in summer. You can reduce the amount of time it takes by positioning your containers in one part of the greenhouse so they can be watered together.

When to water?

Different plants have different watering requirements, and it is essential that you check your plants regularly so that they are watered before they wilt and suffer stress. The simplest way to judge if a plant needs watering is to push your finger into the compost (soil mix) – if it is dry 2cm (¾in) below the surface the container needs watering. You can take a lot of the hard work out of watering by installing an automatic or semi-automatic system.

Automatic watering

Some watering systems allow plants in containers to draw just the right amount of water they need from a reservoir by capillary action. The pots stand on a bed of damp sand or on a special fabric that draws the water from a reservoir. As the plant takes in moisture through its roots, water is drawn up from the bed of sand or capillary matting via capillary action to replenish it. You can make a capillary sand bed out of a sturdy box about 15cm (6in) deep that has been lined with thick black plastic sheeting. Place a 2.5cm (1in) layer of pea gravel inside to provide drainage and cover with a 10cm (4in) layer of horticultural sand. Firm, level and then stand the containers on top.

FEEDING AND WATERING IN THE GREENHOUSE

1 Plants should be watered before they show obvious signs of distress, such as wilting. With bushy plants it is not possible to judge simply by the visual appearance of the compost (soil mix), and touch is usually the best guide. Don't just feel the surface – push your finger down into the compost.

2 Moisture indicators for individual pots, which show when the compost has dried out, can be helpful for a beginner who is uncertain when to water, or if there are just a few plants, but they are not a practical solution if you have a whole greenhouse or conservatory full of plants.

3 Capillary matting is an ideal way to water most pot-plants in summer. You can use a proprietary system fed by mains water or improvise with a system like the one illustrated. This uses a length of gutter for the water supply. You can keep it topped up by hand or plumb it into the mains.

4 If watering by hand, use the can without a rose unless you are watering seedlings. This will enable you to direct water more easily to the roots rather than sprinkling the leaves. Place a finger over the end of the spout to control the flow.

5 Use a liquid fertilizer applied with the water if you can remember to do it regularly. There are both soluble powders and liquids that can be diluted to the appropriate strength. Choose a high-potash feed for fruiting crops such as tomatoes.

6 Fertilizer sticks and tablets that you push into the compost are a convenient way to administer fertilizer if you don't want to apply liquid feeds regularly. Those releasing their nutrients over a period of several months need applying only once.

Watering and feeding are of critical importance throughout the lifetime of greenhouse crops. To achieve good yields from hungry crops, such as tomatoes, you may have to apply a liquid feed every week in addition to watering at least once a day.

Capillary matting is even easier to use. Lay the fabric on a thick sheet of black plastic placed on a level surface. Drape one end of the matting into a trough or short piece of guttering with the ends in place to act as the reservoir. Water the containers thoroughly from above to start the capillary action and keep the reservoir topped up as necessary.

Where a capillary watering system isn't practicable, such as with large containers and growing bags, you could opt for a drip watering system instead. You can buy bladder bags with a single drip nozzle that supplies water rather like a medical drip to individual plants, or you could make your own out of an upturned plastic drinks bottle with the bottom removed. Drill a small hole in the lid and fit a loose galvanized screw into it, then stand the bottle vertically in the compost next to the plant. Any water poured into the bottle will leak out past the screw very slowly – providing water over many hours. Alternatively, you can set up an easy-to-install and reliable micro-bore irrigation system to water your entire greenhouse.

Feeding

Plants vary in the amount and type of nutrients they require. Fast-growing crops in containers will need feeding the most often – perhaps once a week. Tomatoes and cucumbers should be given a high-potash liquid feed. Start feeding tomatoes in early summer once the first truss of flowers has set and stop feeding in late summer once the last truss has set. Start feeding cucumbers in midsummer when the first fruits start to swell. Always follow the manufacturer's instructions on the packet label for application rates.

Looking after greenhouse crops

A greenhouse provides the perfect environment for raising fast-growing tender crops such as tomatoes and cucumbers, but it is also a haven for the pests and diseases that attack them. There are a number of steps you can take to minimize the risks so that your plants grow strongly and crop well. Preventative measures will reduce the need for expensive chemical or biological controls.

Preventing problems

At the end of the growing season the greenhouse should be emptied and carefully cleaned so that pests and diseases cannot overwinter ready to attack the following year's crop. Even at this time of year you can practise good greenhouse hygiene by clearing out any dead or dying material before it becomes a source of infection. You can also make sure your crops are growing strongly so that they can shrug off attacks more easily. Avoid easy access for disease spores by making clean cuts with a sharp, clean blade when you are training your crops.

To get the most from your crops, you also need to be vigilant for problems and take action to control outbreaks quickly. Keep flying pests out of the greenhouse by covering vents and the door with insect-proof mesh and control those inside by hanging up sticky traps among the plants.

Biological controls

Many common greenhouse pests can be tackled by introducing their natural enemies into your greenhouse, a method known as biological control. The greenhouse or conservatory is an ideal place to practise biological control methods – the predators can be kept where they are needed and will thrive in the protected environment where they should multiply rapidly until control is achieved. For example, a parasitic wasp, *Encarsia formosa*, will control whitefly, while a predatory mite called *Phytoseiulus* can be used against spider mite attacks, and nematodes can be used to attack vine weevil larvae. Introduce the biological control as soon as you notice the first sign of the pest. You will need to remove any flying insect traps and stop spraying chemicals that might kill the biological control.

Care of greenhouse crops

Aubergines (eggplants) make bushier plants if the growing tip is pinched out when the plant is about 30cm (12in) high. Allow only one fruit to develop on each shoot. Pinch out the growing tips of these shoots three leaves beyond the developing fruit. Never let the plants dry out, and feed regularly. Mist to provide high humidity which is beneficial.

Melons Train the side shoots of melons to horizontal wires, and pinch back the sideshoots to two leaves beyond each fruit that develops. Melons may require pollinating, in which case transfer the pollen from male to female flowers with a small paintbrush. It may also be necessary to support developing fruits in nets strung from the ceiling.

USING BIOLOGICAL CONTROLS

1 Various forms of biological controls are available for a number of greenhouse pests including red spider mite, soft scale insects, mealybugs and thrips. *Encarsia formosa* is a tiny wasp that parasitizes whitefly larvae.

2 If vine weevil grubs destroy your plants by eating the roots, try controlling them in future with a parasitic eelworm. A suspension of the eelworms is simply watered into the compost (soil mix) in each pot in summer.

Pest and disease patrol

Spider mite Watch out for speckled, yellowing leaves on aubergines (eggplants), cucumbers and melons. Examine the undersides of affected leaves as well as the plants' growing tips where the insects tend to congregate. If attacks are severe, webbing may also be present. This pest likes warm, dry conditions, so ventilate the greenhouse well and damp down surfaces. Try a biological control or spray a suitable systemic insecticide.

White-fly Clouds of tiny white insects rise up when disturbed on crops such as aubergines, peppers and tomatoes. These sap-sucking insects congregate on the undersides of leaves and can be controlled using sticky traps, biological controls or a suitable contact insecticide.

Grey mould (botrytis) Felty patches appear on leaves, fruit and stems. Keep the greenhouse well ventilated and clear away any infected material as well as yellowing leaves to reduce the chances of infection.

Sooty mould This black mould thrives on the sticky deposits left on the surface of leaves low down on the plant after being exuded by sap-sucking insects, such as white-fly and green- and blackfly, higher up. The mould weakens the plant by reducing its ability to photosynthesize. Wipe off with soapy water and control sap-sucking insects.

Aubergines (eggplants) are attacked by a range of common greenhouse pests including aphids, spider mites and whitefly.

SUMMER CARE FOR GREENHOUSE TOMATOES

1 If the plants are supported by strings, simply loop the string around the top of the shoot whenever necessary. It will form a spiral support that holds the stem upright.

2 If the tomato is supported by a vertical bamboo cane, use soft string wound twice around the stake and then loop it loosely around the stem before tying the knot.

3 Snap off side shoots while they are still small. They will snap off cleanly if you pull them sideways. Do not remove side shoots if you have a low-growing bush variety.

4 If fruits are failing to form, poor pollination may be the problem. Shake the plants each day, or spray the flowers with water, to spread the pollen from flower to flower. This is best carried out in the middle of the day.

5 Tomatoes respond well to feeding. Give them regular feeds with a proprietary tomato fertilizer that is high in potash to promote fruit production.

6 The lowest leaves often turn yellow as they age. Remove these, as they will not contribute to feeding the plant, and letting more light reach the fruits can help to ripen them. Snap them cleanly off the stem.

Growing and training vegetables

To keep vegetables growing well, they need to be given room to grow and not allowed to run short of water or nutrients. Most garden soils contain sufficient nutrients to grow most vegetables as long as you apply plenty of well-rotted organic matter when the ground is cultivated. Regular maintenance throughout the summer will ensure optimum cropping.

Feeding vegetables

On poor soils a few hungry crops, such as Brussels sprouts, cabbages, cauliflowers and maincrop potatoes, will need to be given extra feed to do well. This is usually given as a base dressing before the crop is planted, then as a side dressing during the life of the crop. Most soils contain plenty of phosphate and potash, so for leafy crops choose a high-nitrogen fertilizer to boost yields. Potatoes and root crops, on the other hand, will produce a lot of topgrowth at the expense of roots and tubers with this feeding regime, and should be given a fertilizer that is high in phosphate instead. Fruiting crops, such as tomatoes and courgettes (zucchini), do best with a fertilizer that provides a high proportion of

EARTHING UP LEEKS

As the leeks grow, earth (hill) them up by pulling the soil up around the stems to blanch them. This will give the leeks a better flavour.

potash. With such conflicting demands, often the best option is to use a balanced, all-purpose feed, which provides these three major nutrients in equal amounts.

Pest patrol

The best way of keeping pests under control is to ensure your crops are growing well and be vigilant so that you can catch outbreaks early and take appropriate action.

Aphids Blackfly on broad (fava) beans are a common sight and will move to other crops, such as French (green) and runner beans. Other

PROTECTING CAULIFLOWERS

Cauliflowers are sometimes scorched by the hot sun. Protect from discoloration by covering them with the inner leaves.

types of aphids also attack brassicas, courgettes and lettuce. If you garden organically, you may wish to wait for natural predators to bring outbreaks under control, but plants will be weakened and yields lost. Aphids can also spread debilitating viruses, which could destroy the whole crop. However, you can give natural predators a hand by rubbing off early colonies of insects and removing the tips of broad beans on which blackfly congregate. As a last resort, apply a suitable insecticide.

Carrot fly Inconspicuous shiny black flies lay their eggs near the stems of

TRAINING OUTDOOR TOMATOES

1 If you are growing a cordon variety (one that is growing as a single main stem, supported by a cane), keep removing side shoots as they develop in the leaf axil – that is, where the leaf joins the stem.

2 Regular tying in to the support is even more important outdoors than in the greenhouse, because strong winds can break an unsupported stem and shorten the productive life of the plant.

3 As soon as the plant has set the number of trusses (sprays) of fruit likely to be ripened in your area, pinch out the top of the plant. In many areas you can only reasonably expect to ripen four trusses.

BLANCHING CELERY

1 Blanching celery stems makes them taste sweeter. When the stems are 30cm (12in) long, tie them loosely together just below the leaves.

2 Fasten a collar of cardboard around the stems. They will eventually blanch – that is, become white – because of the lack of light.

3 Although soil can also be pulled up around the stems to blanch them, a collar will stop soil from getting into the crown.

carrots and related plants. Grubs hatch and burrow into the roots, ruining the crop. You can prevent this pest by using physical barriers or by sprinkling a suitable soil insecticide into the seed drill before sowing. Late crops sown in early summer will not be affected.

Onion fly This tiny insect lays its eggs next to onions and related crops. The grubs hatch and burrow into the developing bulbs, killing seedlings and ruining larger bulbs. Following a strict crop rotation will help prevent this pest, but you can also apply a suitable soil insecticide to the seedbed before sowing.

Pea moth Adult moths are active in early and midsummer, laying eggs next to the flowers on pea plants. The grubs burrow into the developing pods and eat young peas. Crops sown in early or late spring are less affected than those sown in mid-spring because they flower before or after the time when the adult moths are on the wing. However, you can still usually use the undamaged peas by sorting through the crop at harvest time. The alternative is to apply a preventative spray at flowering time.

Outdoor tomatoes

Tomatoes that have been grown outside need less attention than greenhouse varieties, especially if you grow the kinds on which you leave on the side shoots. Feeding and watering are necessary if you want a good crop of quality fruits. Regular watering not only ensures a heavy crop but also reduces the risk of splitting through uneven watering, which sometimes happens if dry weather

produces hard skins that can't cope with a sudden spurt of growth following a wet period. Add a liquid fertilizer to the water, at the rate and frequency recommended by the manufacturer. How well your crop does depends on a combination of variety, care and climate. In cold areas, outdoor tomatoes can be a disappointing crop, but in warm areas you will almost certainly have more fruit than you can eat.

Outdoor tomatoes require less attention than those grown indoors and if trained using inconspicuous supports, can look attractive in a prominent position.

Harvesting and storing herbs

Herbs can be picked for culinary use at any time during the growing season, and a few, such as thyme, can be harvested in small amounts during the autumn and winter too. If you want to harvest herbs for drying and storing, the best time will depend on the part of the plant you want to collect: leaves, flowers, roots or seeds.

Harvesting

All herbs should be picked when they are in their prime. Avoid old, diseased

HARVESTING HERBS

Harvest herbs when they are at their peak, usually before they flower. Cut them on a dry day, avoiding times when they are wilting in the heat. Harvest the best leaves, not the older leaves lower down the plant.

or discoloured parts, and try to pick in the morning after the dew has evaporated but before the sun has dissipated the essential oils that give herbs their distinctive taste and aroma. Don't be tempted to pick wet herbs for drying and storing because these are more likely to go mouldy. Cut the material cleanly from the parent plant using a sharp pair of scissors or secateurs (pruners). Avoid collecting large batches of herbs all at once, because there will inevitably be a delay before some are prepared for storage. Heaps of unprepared herbs are likely to heat up and deteriorate.

Leafy herbs should be picked before the plants come into flower. This is the stage when their essential oils are at their most concentrated and producing the best aroma and flavour. Small-leaved herbs, such as thyme and rosemary, should be picked on the stem, while the leaves of large-leaved herbs, such as bay, can be picked individually off the parent plant. Flowers are best harvested as they start to open — pick single blooms or whole flowerheads as appropriate. Seeds are best picked as soon as they are ripe

Collect herbs, like this marjoram, when they are at their best. Small-leaved herbs should be picked attached to the stem, while larger-leaved herbs can be picked as individual leaves.

(when the pod has turned from green to brown), and roots are usually removed while the plant is dormant during the winter months.

Drying

Leafy herbs dry best in a well-ventilated place that's dark and warm — an airing cupboard is ideal. Aim for a temperature of 35°C (95°F), although anything above 20°C (68°F) will do. Hang the herbs up

HARVESTING MARJORAM FOR DRYING

1 Small-leaved herbs, such as marjoram, are easily air-dried. Cut bunches of healthy material at mid-morning on a dry, warm day.

2 Strip off the lower leaves, which would otherwise become crushed and damaged when the stems are bunched.

3 Twist a rubber band around a few stems to hold them tightly together. Gather as many bunches as you need.

DRYING HERB SEEDS

1 Pick seedheads just as they are ripening. At this stage the seeds should readily come away from the stalks. Place them on a tray and leave the seeds for a few days in a warm, dry place until they have completely dried.

2 Make sure that the seeds are completely dry and then sieve them to remove any debris and bits of seed husks before putting them into a glass jar with an airtight lid. Label clearly and store in a cool, dry, dark place.

FREEZING HERBS

The best method of storing soft-leaved herbs, such as parsley and mint, is to freeze them. Chop up the leaves and place them in ice-cube trays. Top up with water and freeze. This helps maintain the herb's colour.

in bunches or lay them in open racks so that they dry quickly and thoroughly. Within a week the herbs should be so dry that they rustle. Strip the leaves from their stems and store each herb in individual airtight containers. Seedpods are best dried in paper bags to catch the seed.

Storing

The best way to store dry herbs is in clearly labelled, airtight opaque containers so that they are protected from direct light. Better still, keep

them in a dark cupboard. Herbs can also be preserved in herb oils and vinegars, which have many culinary uses. You can create single flavours or mixed herbs to taste. This is a good way to store herbs such as basil that do not dry well. Other soft-leaved herbs, such as parsley and mint, can be stored frozen in ice cubes, which helps preserve their flavour and colour. The ice cube can then be added to summer drinks or used in stews and casseroles as required. Whole sprigs of other

herbs can also be frozen for winter use. Either wrap them in foil or lay them on trays to freeze.

Herb mixtures

Different herbs can be combined in a number of distinctive mixtures. *Bouquet garni,* for example, is a combination of several herbs, such as bay, parsley, marjoram and thyme. Sprigs of the herbs are tied together or placed in a muslin (cheesecloth) bag, which is cooked with the dish and removed before serving.

Herbs to dry

Bay	Lemon verbena
Caraway	Mint
Clary	Rosemary
Coriander	Sage
Dill	Savory
Fennel	Tarragon
Lemon balm	Thyme

Herbs to freeze

Basil	Lovage
Borage	Marjoram
Coriander	Mint
Dill	Parsley
Lemon balm	Rosemary

DRYING HERBS

Bunches of herbs can be dried by hanging them in a dry, well-ventilated place where they are out of direct sunlight.

HERB MIXTURES

Grow herbs in individual pots, which can be kept in a larger container and replaced when the plants are past their best.

Summer pruning trained fruit trees

Shaped and trained apple trees are normally pruned twice a year – once in summer and again in winter. Summer pruning controls the amount of growth produced each year and maintains the basic shape; winter pruning consists of thinning overcrowded fruiting spurs on old plants. In late spring the new growth at the ends of the main shoots is cut back to its point of origin, but summer pruning is the most crucial in terms of maintaining the trained shape.

Pruning apples and pears

On trained forms of apples and pears, all mature new shoots that originate directly from the main trunk and are over 23 cm (9 in) long should be cut back to three leaves once extension growth is complete.

SUMMER PRUNING ESPALIER APPLES

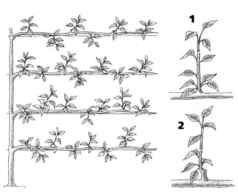

1 Shorten new leafy shoots that have grown directly from the main branches back to three leaves above the basal cluster of leaves. This should be done only once the shoots have dark green leaves and the bark has started to turn brown and is woody at the base. In cold areas it may be early autumn before the shoots are mature enough.

2 If the shoot is growing from a stub left by previous pruning – and not directly from one of the main stems – cut back to just one leaf above the basal cluster of leaves.

SUMMER PRUNING CORDON APPLES

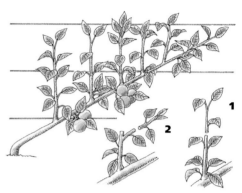

1 A cordon is pruned in exactly the same way as an espalier, although, of course, the basic shape of the plant is different. Just cut back shoots growing directly from the main branch to three leaves above the basal cluster of leaves.

2 Cut back shoots growing from stubs left by earlier pruning to one leaf above the basal cluster. Well-established trees may become congested with fruiting clusters, so these may need thinning periodically.

Pears grown as cordons are a space-efficient way of growing fruit in a small garden. If correctly pruned, heavy crops can be produced from a single row of trees.

This does not include the clusters of leaves found at the base of such shoots. All mature shoots that originate from the sideshoots (laterals) on the main trunk should be cut back to one leaf beyond the cluster of leaves at their base. If the new shoots have not turned brown at the base and are easily bent when pulled downwards from the tip they are not sufficiently mature and should be left until late summer or early autumn before they are pruned. Always use sharp secateurs (pruners) or a pruning knife so that cuts are able to heal quickly, reducing the risk of disease attack.

Summer pruning other fruits

Grapes Outside, prune side shoots (laterals) carrying bunches of developing grapes back to two leaves from the supporting wire. Subsequent new shoots (sub-laterals) should be cut back to one leaf. Allow one truss to develop per lateral during the early years, increasing to two or three per lateral once well established. All unwanted growth should be removed back to the main framework of stems. Alternatively, train using the traditional guyot system described below. In the greenhouse, pinch out non-fruiting laterals after they have developed six leaves and sub-laterals to just one leaf.

Figs Figs grown as free-standing bushes should have the tip of each new shoot pinched out after five leaves to encourage new fruit-bearing shoots to form lower down the stems. Trained forms of figs should have half of their new side shoots (laterals) cut back in this way. These will bear fruit next year. If grown in an unheated greenhouse, prune the side shoots back to just above the fourth leaf and in a heated greenhouse prune back to two leaves.

Peaches On trained forms prune out any laterals that are pointing in the wrong direction, such as towards the wall support, to maintain the overall shape. Also, after harvest, cut back fruited laterals to a replacement lateral lower down. Tie in new shoots to the supporting framework.

Trained forms of apples and pears make attractive and productive garden dividers that don't take up too much space.

SUMMER PRUNING GRAPES

Train new shoots vertically, removing any side shoots that develop on them to one leaf. Allow vertical fruiting shoots to grow on the horizontal branches, removing any side shoots. Cut back above the top wire to three leaves.

SUMMER PRUNING FIGS

Pinch out the growing tips of about half of the young shoots that are carried on the main framework branches. You should do this towards the end of midsummer. As the shoots develop, tie them to the wires.

SUMMER PRUNING COBNUTS

Late summer Established trees should be pruned in late summer. Strong lateral growths are broken off by hand to about six to eight leaves from the base and left to hang.

Harvesting and storing vegetables

The harvest season is now in full swing on the vegetable patch, and you will be kept busy picking and digging up a wide range of crops, probably every day. Some of them you will want to use immediately, while you will be storing others to enjoy through the colder months. You can use the following as a guide to make the most of your labours.

Aubergine (eggplant)

Cut the fruit from the plant using a sharp knife when it's ripe and fully coloured – the flavour quickly deteriorates if they are allowed to become over-ripe. Store fruits for up to two months or cut each fruit in half, or peel and dice, before blanching and then freezing.

Broccoli and calabrese

Harvest broccoli on a 10cm (4in) stalk when the heads have formed but the flowers are still in tight bud. Calabrese can be cut with a 2.5cm (1in) stalk when the main central head is still firm with tight buds. Leave plants to grow on and produce side shoots to be harvested later. Regular harvesting encourages better yields. Eat fresh or blanch and freeze.

Corn

Check that the cobs are ripe when the silky tassels start to turn brown. Press a thumbnail into individual grains on the cob until the juice is released. If it is clear and watery leave to ripen further, if creamy it

STORING GARLIC

A simple way of "stringing" garlic is to thread a stiff wire through the dry necks of the bulbs. The bulbs can also be tied on string.

is ready to harvest. Pick each cob individually by holding the main plant firmly and twisting the cob free. Eat fresh or blanch and freeze.

Courgettes (zucchini)

Remove young fruits from the plant when they are 10–15cm (4–6in) long. Do not allow them to get any larger, otherwise the plant will stop producing new fruit. They should be eaten fresh, but will remain in good condition in a refrigerator for about a week after harvest. Alternatively, slice and freeze for later use.

French (green) beans

Harvest when young and crisp, usually when they are about 10cm (4in) long. Do not leave old beans on the plant, or subsequent yields will be reduced. You should pick over the plants regularly. Hold the stem of the plant as you pick to prevent it being ripped out of the ground. Eat fresh or trim, blanch and freeze.

Onions

When leaves topple in late summer, the crop is reaching maturity. Do not bend the leaves over, but let the crop dry out and go dormant

RIPENING AND HARVESTING ONIONS

1 The traditional practice of bending the leaves of onions over is no longer recommended as it encourages diseases in storage. Let the foliage die down naturally.

2 As soon as the foliage has turned a straw colour and is brittle, lift the onions with a fork and leave them on the surface with their roots facing the sun for a few days to dry off.

3 To complete the ripening process place the bulbs on wire mesh supported above the ground so that air can circulate freely.

4 If the weather is damp, cover the bulbs with cloches until you can store them. Use damaged bulbs first.

HARVESTING SQUASH

Harvest a courgette (zucchini), marrow (large zucchini) or other squash by cutting it off right at the base with a sharp knife.

HARVESTING RUNNER BEANS

Harvest runner beans when they are large enough but still fresh and pliable; discard the older, tougher beans.

HARVESTING TOMATOES

Harvest tomatoes when they are fully ripe, which will usually be when they turn red. Leave the stalks on.

naturally. Once the foliage is dry and brown, lift the crop and move on to drying racks for at least a week. Outdoors is best if the weather is dry and sunny, but if it rains they should be moved to a well-ventilated place under cover. In wet years, it may be necessary to cover the row with cloches to help them dry out before moving them indoors.

Potatoes

Wait until the topgrowth has started to die down on maincrop potatoes before lifting. Cut off the remaining foliage and leave the crop for two weeks so that the tubers mature. Before you harvest, excavate at the side of the row to make sure the tubers are sufficiently mature and that their skins do not rub off. Harvest when the weather and soil are dry and store dry in paper sacks.

Shallots

If planted early, these can be lifted in midsummer. If you planted late it may be late summer before they are ready to harvest. Lift the bulbs in dry weather when the leaves die back. Wait for a week for the bulbs to ripen and the remaining foliage to

dry. Store only perfect bulbs in nets or trays, or strung up together.

Runner beans

Pick beans while they are small and tender. Harvest regularly so that you do not leave old beans on the plant, which will slow the production of new flowers and pods and reduce subsequent yields. Eat fresh or blanch and freeze.

Tomatoes

The first fruits ripen two to three months after planting. Harvest fruit when it is fully ripened and starting to soften, by gently lifting the fruit and breaking it from the truss at its "knuckle joint". Eat fresh or freeze.

Turnip and swede (rutabaga)

Leave in the ground until needed. Then lift individual roots carefully.

It is essential that onions and shallots are completely dry before they are stored. Place them in trays or nets in a cool but frost-free place.

Harvesting and storing fruit

Harvest fruit when it is in prime condition, taking care not to damage it because this will encourage storage rots later on. Fruit for storing dry should be picked slightly under-ripe, while crops for bottling or freezing are best fully ripe, but not over-ripe. As soon as the fruit is harvested, transfer it to somewhere cool and complete the storing process as quickly after harvest as possible.

Storage methods

The easiest way to store fruit is to freeze it. To help retain flavour, it is best to freeze in layers of dry sugar or in syrup. However, soft fruit can be frozen dry on open trays before being bagged or boxed. Making surplus fruit into sweet preserves is another option. The pectin in the fruit gels with the sugar and acid to thicken the preserve and bacteria cannot survive in the sugary environment.

Apples and pears Harvest when slightly under-ripe but when the fruit comes away from the branch with its stalk intact when you gently lift and twist. Trees will need picking over several times to harvest the fruit

in the right state for storage. Fruit exposed to direct sun will ripen first and shaded fruit last. Choose perfect, average-sized fruits to store. Large fruits tend to rot more easily in storage and small fruits tend to shrivel. Different varieties store for different periods, so keep them separate in the store. Keep in a cool, frost-free place so that the fruits are not touching – special moulded paper trays in ventilated cardboard

boxes are ideal. Inspect fruits regularly and remove any that are showing signs of deterioration. Apples and pears can also be bottled, frozen or puréed.

Blackberries Pick slightly under-ripe for freezing and fully ripe for eating fresh or turning into jam.

Blackcurrants Pick the fruit complete with stalk when the berries are fully coloured. Eat fresh or turn into jam.

Storing apples and pears

Apples	Harvest time	Store until
'Cox's Orange Pippin'	early autumn	late winter
'Discovery'	late summer	eat fresh
'Egremont Russet'	early autumn	midwinter
'Greensleeves'	early autumn	late winter
'Grenadier'	late summer	early autumn
'Idared'	mid-autumn	early spring
'James Grieve'	early autumn	eat fresh
'Jupiter'	early autumn	late winter
'Katja'	late summer	late autumn
'Laxton's Superb'	late autumn	midspring
'Sunset'	early autumn	midwinter
'Worcester Pearmain'	early autumn	early winter
Pears		
'Conference'	mid-autumn	late winter
'Doyenné du Comice'	early autumn	early winter

STORING APPLES

Apples can be stored in trays in a cool, dry place. It is best if they are laid in individual screws of paper or moulded paper trays so that the individual fruits do not touch. The length of storage time depends on the variety.

STORING SOFT FRUIT

Soft fruit such as raspberries and hybrid berries is best placed in small individual containers as it is picked to prevent it being squashed and spoiling. Store in a refrigerator or other cool place.

STORING PEARS

Pears can last many months depending upon the variety. Lay them in a box so that the fruits do not touch and air can circulate around them. The best varieties for storage are 'Conference' and 'Doyenné du Comice'.

Cherries Easier to harvest in the early morning when fully ripe, with the stalk intact to prevent the fruit bleeding. Eat fresh or remove stones (pits) before bottling or freezing.

Gooseberries Pick while still under-ripe and green for bottling and freezing, but wait until fully ripe and softening slightly for eating fresh.

Grapes Harvest grapes when they are ripe by removing the whole bunch from the vine along with a little of the woody vine on each side of the bunch using a pair or scissors or secateurs (pruners). Eat fresh.

Peaches and nectarines Gently twist the fruit as it rests in the palm of your hand to see if it is ready to pick. Ripe fruit will be well coloured and softening slightly near the stalk. Eat fresh, freeze or bottle.

Plums Harvest when fully ripe if eating fresh, slightly under-ripe for cooking and preserving. Pick with stalk intact. Halve and stone (pit) before bottling or making into jam.

Raspberries Pick when fully coloured but still firm to the touch when each fruit is easily detached from its "plug". For larger hybrid berries, harvest with scissors to remove the fruits complete with their stalks. Eat fresh, freeze or turn into jam.

Red and white currants Pick when ripe by removing the whole strings of fruit. Remove stalks before eating fresh, freezing or turning into jam.

Strawberries Harvest when the fruit is fully coloured but still firm. Pick by holding the fruit in the palm of your hand while pinching the stalk off between finger and thumb. Eat fresh or turn into jam.

Apricots When fully ripened, the fruit can be picked cleanly from its stalk. Eat fresh, dry or freeze.

HARVESTING APPLES AND PEARS

Apples and pears are removed from the tree with a twist of the wrist. The stalks should remain attached to the fruit.

Blueberries Pick when ripe and fully coloured. Eat fresh or freeze.

Nuts Filberts and cobnuts should be picked when the husk starts to turn yellow. Eat them fresh or dry and store.

Harvesting soft fruit and plums for storage

Blackberries	Harvest time
'Bedford Giant'	midsummer
'Oregon Thornless'	late summer

Blackcurrants	
'Ben Lomond'	midsummer
'Malling Jet'	late summer

Gooseberries	
'Careless'	early summer
'Leveller'	early summer

Plums	
'Czar'	midsummer
'Early Rivers'	midsummer
'Oullin's Golden Gage'	late summer
'Victoria'	late summer

Raspberries	
'Glen Clova'	early summer
'Malling Admiral'	midsummer
'Malling Delight'	early summer
'Malling Jewel'	early summer
'Malling Leo'	midsummer

Apples should be picked over several times during late summer and early autumn to make sure that each one is harvested at exactly the right stage of maturity.

Autumn

Autumn can be an Indian summer or the first taste of winter, so you will need to keep a close eye on weather forecasts. Be watchful and vigilant as the nights become colder. In some areas quite severe frosts are common in early autumn, and in others light frosts may not occur until mid- or late autumn, if at all. You can extend the harvest period by covering with cloches outdoor crops such as lettuce so that they continue to grow and tomatoes so that they have time to ripen before the first serious frost. In the greenhouse you can sow some winter lettuce, and keep a few pots of herbs under cover. Parsley can be sown outdoors for a winter harvest. Most tender crops will be harvested by early autumn and any surplus carefully stored for winter use. If you grow a lot of vegetables from seed, you can save money by saving your own seed from selected plants that have been allowed to flower and set seed. In the established fruit garden, this is a good time to carry out many pruning tasks.

Root vegetables, leeks and Brussels sprouts are the mainstay of the kitchen garden during the autumn months.

Extending your harvests

If you have cloches that you normally use to protect your crops in spring, make the most of them by extending the end of the season as well as the beginning. They can be used to get late sowings off to a flying start as well as to help extend the productive life of tender crops by protecting them from early frosts.

Practical matters

Late sowings of quick-growing crops, such as lettuce 'Little Gem', can be grown on quickly under cloches for a late autumn harvest, while hardy crops, such as early carrots, summer cauliflowers and peas, can be started now under

cloches and overwintered to be ready to harvest well before their spring-sown counterparts. This is the traditional way of filling the gap between the last of this year's crops and the first of those sown next spring. Other crops to try include broad (fava) beans, early calabrese and leaf beet. Some hardy crops, such as spinach and endive, also benefit from protection if an early frost threatens. Again, use spare cloches or cover with a double layer of garden fleece to insulate against the cold.

Save large barn cloches for large crops such as tomatoes, and use tent and plastic tunnel cloches for low-growing crops such as lettuce.

PROTECTING OUTDOOR TOMATOES

1 Frost will kill tomatoes, but you can often extend their season and ripen a few more fruits on the plant with protection. Low-growing bush plants can be insulated with a bed of straw and covered with a large cloche.

2 Cordon-trained tomatoes must be lowered before they can be protected. Remove the growing tip, any ripe fruit and yellowing leaves, then untie the plant from its support and remove the stake.

3 Lay a bed of straw on the ground and lower the plants on to this. If you lay all the stems in the same direction, you will have a neat row of tomatoes that can be easily covered with cloches. Remove ripe fruit every day.

4 Fleece can be used to offer wind protection and enough shelter to keep off a degree or two of frost, though it does not warm the air during the day in the same way that glass or other rigid materials will do.

CUTTING DOWN ASPARAGUS HAULMS

In the autumn, as the asparagus fronds are turning brown, cut them down to about 2.5cm (1in) above ground level. Apply a mulch of well-rotted compost along the trench to replenish the soil for the next season.

Cordon tomatoes can be untied from the supports and laid horizontally on a bed of straw so that they too can be covered with cloches for the last few weeks. Green tomatoes can be ripened indoors if they have reached a reasonable stage of maturity. If left on the plant, harvest as soon as a severe frost is forecast.

Saving your own seed

If you grow a lot of vegetables each year, it might be worth leaving a few plants of each crop to mature and set seed so that they can be collected and stored ready for next year. On fruiting crops, such as tomatoes, you need only save one or two fruit to ripen fully, while with peas it's a matter of leaving a few pods on the plant at harvest time. Bear in mind that with beans, which need to be picked regularly to ensure a continuous crop, leaving pods to mature on a plant will slow the rate of new pod development and so reduce overall yields. So wait until the end of the season to leave a few pods to mature and choose the most productive plant. Collect the fruits when they are fully ripe and starting

PUTTING CLOCHES IN PLACE

1 Winter and mooli (daikon) radishes are frost-hardy, but to encourage further growth before bad weather sets in, cover with cloches. If not already sown, start off under cloches in a mild area, provided the soil is still warm.

2 Try sowing lamb's lettuce and winter purslane as a cold weather crop. They don't need cloche protection except in cold areas, but the cover will ensure a better supply of more succulent leaves.

3 Put the cloches in position over the rows before the cold weather has had time to check growth. With only a little protection like this the plants will crop more freely and over a much longer period.

to soften (tomatoes and marrows) or have dried out and become hard (peas and beans).

With crops that are normally picked before they flower, such as lettuce, root crops and brassicas, you'll have to leave at least two plants of the same variety to mature and flower. Two are normally required because their flowers need to cross-pollinate to set seed. You may have to wait until the following year before this happens with brassicas and crops in the onion family.

Planting garlic

You can plant garlic from the supermarket, if it looks healthy, but varieties sold for gardeners are more likely to succeed, especially in cooler climates. Garlic needs a cool period before it sprouts in spring so it can be planted any time during autumn and winter. Prepare the ground by thoroughly digging and removing weeds, and on poor soils rake in a base dressing of general fertilizer, about two weeks before planting. Any time after the weather conditions

turn cold in your area you can plant garlic cloves; this is usually in early autumn in the coldest areas, and in late autumn in milder gardens. Plant on ridges to aid drainage if your soil is heavy. Use a dibber or small trowel to plant the cloves 10–15cm (4–6in) apart, using a garden line as a guide. Plant vertically with the pointed tip facing upwards in holes twice the depth of the clove.

PLANTING GARLIC

1 Use a dibber to make holes in the ground for each clove, at 10–15cm (4–6in) intervals. A line of string held on two pegs will help you to keep the row straight.

2 Plant the cloves just below the surface of the ground so that the bulbs are upright, firming them in so that they are covered to their own height with soil.

Harvesting will be peaking by early autumn, but you can extend the cropping period of many outdoor vegetables by taking action to protect them now.

Storing vegetables

One of the biggest challenges when growing vegetables is making sure that harvested crops can be kept in tip-top condition until they are needed in the kitchen. Fortunately, many vegetables are easy to store either in the ground where they are growing or in a frost-free shed or garage. Most of those that don't store well can be blanched and frozen, or preserved in other ways.

Storing outside

Most root crops, including carrots, swedes (rutabagas) and turnips, as well as hardy vegetables such as leeks and Brussels sprouts, can be left in the ground until they are needed. If you have light soil, root crops can be left in position all winter without deteriorating. Mark the rows with canes or labels so that you know where to dig after the topgrowth has died down. If you live in an area that is prone to hard frosts, you will need to protect the vegetables with an insulating layer of straw held in place with netting, so that you can harvest the crops successfully even when the soil is frozen solid. The main disadvantages of leaving the crop in the ground are that they may have to be harvested when the soil is very wet or frozen, and you'll inevitably suffer winter losses from pest and disease attacks.

Storing inside in sand

On heavy soil in cold areas, digging up vegetables may be difficult or impossible for much of the winter. In this case, it is best to lift the root crops in autumn when the soil and weather conditions are favourable and keep them in trays or boxes of moist sand in a frost-free shed or garage. Less hardy crops, such as beetroot (beet), will need to be

TRADITIONAL POTATO STORAGE

1 Lift the tubers with a fork once the foliage has died down. Leave the potatoes on the surface for a couple of hours so that the skins dry off and harden. Do not leave them overnight or slugs will damage the tubers.

2 Sort the potatoes before storing them. It is sufficient to grade them into four sizes: very small, small, medium and large. Use the smallest ones immediately and only store the medium and largest sizes.

3 Place the largest potatoes in sacks, seal to exclude light, and store in a cool but frost-proof place. If you can't get paper sacks, use black plastic sacks. Make slits in these for ventilation, but keep away from light.

4 If you have a large crop, make a traditional clamp in the garden. Line a shallow depression with a layer of straw at least 10cm (4in) thick.

5 Pile on the potatoes carefully, then heap a thick layer of straw over the top. It must be thick enough to provide good insulation.

6 Mound earth over the straw, but leave a few tufts of straw sticking out of the top. These will allow a little ventilation.

One of the problems of a productive vegetable plot is how to avoid wasteful gluts. Be prepared for the harvest season so that all the vegetables are picked and stored in the peak of condition.

stored in this way. Choose only the best roots to store and make sure they are not damaged because this will encourage storage rots to develop. Remove the leaves before storage, twisting off beetroot foliage rather than cutting it to reduce bleeding. Lay the roots horizontally in layers of damp sand so that they do not dry out. Use up the smallest roots first.

Storing inside in sacks

Potatoes, on the other hand, should be stored in dry, dark and frost-free conditions. It is essential to keep them in the dark, otherwise they will go green and become inedible. The best option is to place them in special double-skinned paper sacks, which can be tied at the top to exclude light. Then make sure the temperature in your store never falls below freezing. You can help prevent damage from cold by insulating the sacks with sheets of polystyrene (styrofoam) and by laying them on old wooden pallets to improve air circulation. If storage space is limited, you could try using the traditional clamping method. It looks primitive but works well except where winters are very severe.

Storing inside in jars

Crops such as beans and peas can be kept dry in airtight containers such as old jam jars. Make sure the crop is fully ripe and the pods are brittle before removing the dry seeds and storing them in labelled containers.

Storing inside in nets

A few crops, such as onions, marrows and cabbages, are better stored in nets. They will need to be kept in a cool, well-ventilated area that is frost-free and dry during the winter months. Netting bags and old tights (pantyhose) are both suitable, or you could try your hand at braiding members of the onion family into ropes. These crops can also be stored successfully in open trays, provided they are kept well ventilated.

Overwintering herbs

Gathering fresh herbs from the garden allows you to enjoy them at their best, and if you plan ahead you can ensure a regular supply all winter long. A few shrubby herbs, such as rosemary and bay, can be cropped all year without special protection. However, because they are borderline hardy it would be best to grow them in containers in colder areas so that they can be moved inside in winter. Alternatively, cover them with garden fleece during cold spells.

Keeping herbs going

Perennial herbs, such as chives, mint and oregano, which would naturally die down in autumn, can be kept growing much longer by covering selected plants with cloches. In milder areas you might be able to keep them growing all winter using this technique. Evergreen herbs, such as thyme and sage, can also be encouraged if they are protected to continue growing to provide useful material for the kitchen throughout the winter months.

In colder areas it is worth potting up a few herbs if you can keep them somewhere frost-free throughout the winter. An insulated coldframe, greenhouse, conservatory or porch would be ideal, but you could also keep a pot or two growing on a cool bedroom windowsill. Lift the plants complete with roots and soil and transfer to a large pot. If you lift sufficient to fill several pots of each herb you will be able to use them in succession, so that the first has a chance to put on more growth before you revisit it. Vigorous growers, such as mint, can be grown from a few fleshy roots planted into a pot or seed tray of compost (soil mix). Keep moist until shoots appear, then place in a well-lit spot.

A few herbs, including parsley and chervil, can be sown late under protection to provide late winter pickings. Sow in containers of fresh compost and keep them outside until

POTTING UP HERBS FOR WINTER USE

1 Mint is an easy plant to force indoors, or in a coldframe or greenhouse, because it is naturally vigorous. Lift an established clump to provide a supply of roots to pot up.

2 Be careful to select only pieces with healthy leaves (diseased leaves are common by the end of the season). You can pull pieces off by hand or cut through them with a knife.

3 Plant the roots in a pot if you want to try to keep the plant growing indoors for a month or so longer. Lift an entire plant and rootball to supply leaves for longer.

4 If you want a supply of tender fresh leaves early next spring, cut off the tops and put the roots in seed trays or deeper boxes, then cover them with soil. Keep them in a greenhouse or even a protected coldframe.

5 Chives also respond favourably to lifting for an extended season. Lift a small clump complete with rootball and soil to pot up. If it's too large, you should be able to pull it apart into smaller pieces.

6 Place the clump in a pot of ordinary soil or potting compost (soil mix), firm well, and water. It should continue to provide leaves after those outdoors have died back, and will produce new ones earlier next spring.

PROTECTING SWISS CHARD

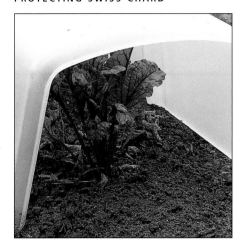

In cold areas, Swiss chard needs some form of winter protection. Any form of cloche or portable coldframe can be used.

CUTTING BACK GLOBE ARTICHOKES

Cut down all stems to ground level when the plant dies back in the autumn. Replace plants after three or, at most, four years.

HARVESTING LEEKS

Harvest the leeks by digging under them with a garden fork. As you do this, pull them out of the ground with the other hand.

temperatures start to drop at night. Pot up the seedlings when they are large enough to handle and place them in a coldframe or greenhouse or on the kitchen windowsill to keep them growing throughout the autumn and winter. They will then provide useful harvests from midwinter onwards.

Some herbs, including borage, fennel and tarragon, cannot be overwintered using these methods and so will need to be frozen or dried if you want to use them during the winter months.

Straw protection

Vegetables such as celery and beetroot (beet) also benefit from protection in cold areas. Pack straw among and between the plants in the blocks or rows. It does not matter if the tops of the leaves are exposed – you are only protecting the edible part. Mature celery will usually survive some frost, but the straw protection is useful if it turns very cold before you are ready to lift it. In mild areas beetroot can be left unprotected, but the straw does help to keep plants in better condition for longer in cold areas.

Protect Swiss chard with cloches or garden fleece during the autumn for the best quality growth, especially in gardens that experience penetrating frosts.

Making compost

Making garden compost allows you to mimic the natural recycling of organic matter that occurs in the soil. It is also a convenient way of getting rid of a lot of bulky waste, and saves you money because you do not have to buy in so much organic matter to boost the fertility of your plot. Making your own compost is, therefore, good for the wider environment, your soil and the plants you are trying to grow.

What you need

You do not need any special equipment to compost successfully. Just pile the material up in a heap and it will eventually break down at the centre. However, to get the compost to break down evenly in the shortest possible time, you would be better off buying or making a compost bin. Aim for the largest size that you have room for: the greater the volume, the more quickly the compost will break down. A bin holding 1 cubic metre (35 cubic feet) is ideal, but smaller sizes can also work well. If you have a large garden that produces a lot of waste, build three bins side by side, so that one can be filled while the second is rotting down and the third is being emptied of well-rotted compost.

Traditionally, compost bins are made from scrap wood, but this rots with the heap and so needs replacing every few years. Making a bin from wood, however, does allow you to build it to fit the space you have available. You can buy manufactured bins that have been pressure-treated against rot so that they last a lot longer. Most ready-made bins, however, are made from plastic. Make sure your ready-made bin is large enough for your needs and has some ventilation (you may need to drill some holes), and that it is easy to access the compost once it is ready for use.

What you can compost

You can recycle virtually any organic waste from the garden or kitchen in a compost bin, but for the composting process to be completed as quickly as possible you will need to mix the different types of material in the bin. You can do this either by mixing the dry and moist ingredients before they are added to the compost heap, or by adding them unmixed in alternate layers not more than 15cm (6in) thick. Dry ingredients include old newspaper and straw and moist ingredients

MAKING COMPOST

1 A simple compost bin, which should be up to 1m (3ft) square and deep, can be made using cheap, pressure-treated fencing timber, or by nailing four flat pallets together.

2 Pile the waste into the bin, taking care that there are no thick layers of one material. Grass clippings will not rot down if the layer is too thick because air cannot penetrate.

3 It is important to keep the compost bin covered with an old mat or a sheet of plastic. This will help to keep in the heat generated by the composting process, prevent it from cooling down too much in winter and also stop the compost from getting too wet, which slows down the process.

4 After about a month, turn the contents of the compost bin with a fork to let in air and to move the outside material, which is slow to rot, into the centre to speed up the composting process. If you have several bins, it is easier to turn the compost by transferring it from one bin into another.

5 When the bin is full, you may want to cover the surface with a layer of soil and use it to grow marrows (large zucchini), pumpkins or cucumbers. If you want to use the contents as soon as possible, remove one of the sides for access. Otherwise, keep the compost covered with plastic or an old piece of carpet.

USING COMPOST IN THE GARDEN

1 Organic material such as well-rotted garden compost or farmyard manure is high in nutrients. Fork in when the soil is dug. For heavy soils, this is best done now.

2 If the soil has already been dug, the organic material can be lightly forked in or left on the surface. The worms will complete the task of working it into the soil.

3 In autumn, and again in spring, top-dress established plants with a layer of well-rotted organic material. This will also help to suppress weeds and conserve soil moisture.

include grass clippings and annual weeds. Any woody materials, such as prunings, should be chopped up with secateurs (pruners) or processed through a garden shredder before being added. Don't include any diseased plant material, and never add meat, fish, fat or other cooked foods, which will attract vermin.

Perennial weed roots and annual weeds that are setting seed might survive the composting process and be spread around your garden when the compost is used. You can use them in the compost if you first leave them to rot in a bucket of water; otherwise, throw them away or bury them deeply in a specially prepared trench.

Composting efficiently

Even when you have the right size bin and the right mixture of ingredients, there is a lot you can do to help it compost more efficiently. The first trick is to give the heap a kick-start by adding a proprietary compost activator or a spadeful of well-rotted compost from a previous bin each time you add a new layer of material to the bin. This will introduce the right microbes as well

as providing them with the perfect environment to work efficiently. Do not allow the heap to dry out or get too wet (which will slow down the composting process) and cover it with a lid in winter to help retain heat within the heap. To ensure the heap composts evenly it will need to be turned after a month. It should

produce sweet-smelling, crumbly, fibrous compost in just a few months in summer and around six months in winter.

If the compost does get too wet, empty the bin completely and then return the compost while mixing in a dry material, such as shredded newspaper, as you go.

Woody material can be added to the compost heap but it needs to be chopped up finely beforehand so that it rots down quickly.

Planning a soft fruit garden

Growing soft fruit is easy provided you choose problem-free varieties, plant them in a suitable position and give them the right sort of care. Indeed, most will reward you with regular crops for many years for the minimum of effort once they are established. The secret, therefore, is to choose the right fruits and grow them in the right way.

Preparing the site

Most soft fruits need to be grown in a sunny site; you can grow red and white currants in a shady area, but yields will be lower. Prepare the site for new soft fruit crops by digging the soil thoroughly and removing all

Most soft fruit requires a sunny site that's sheltered from cold winds to produce good crops. Blackberries and hybrid berries are the exception to this rule, since they will grow equally well in sun or semi-shade. They must have well-drained soil, however.

SUPPORTING CANE FRUIT

1 Knock a strong post well into the ground at the end of the row of cane fruit. It may be easier to dig a hole and insert the post before backfilling and ramming down the earth. Make sure the post is vertical.

2 Knock in another post at an angle of 45 degrees to the vertical to act as a support to the upright post. Nail firmly, using galvanized nails, so that the upright post is rigid and will support the tension of tight wires.

3 Fasten the wires around one end post and pull tight along the row, stapling them to each vertical post. Keep the wires as taut as possible. If necessary, use eye bolts on the end posts to tension the wires.

4 Fasten the canes – in this case raspberry canes – to the wires with string or plant ties. Space the canes out evenly along the wires so that the maximum amount of light can reach the leaves and so that air circulates freely.

perennial weeds. Add as much well-rotted organic matter as you can – ideally to a depth of 5–10cm (2–4in) – to improve the soil structure and fertility.

Blackcurrants

Choose a sheltered, frost-free position so that the early flowers are not damaged by frost; alternatively, choose a late-flowering variety. Blackcurrants are grown as individual bushes spaced 1.5–1.8m (5–6ft) apart, or you can grow them as a hedge, spacing them 90cm (3ft) apart in the row. Cut down all shoots to within 25cm (12in) of the ground after planting. Good varieties include 'Ben Lomond' and 'Ben Sarek'. Choose well-balanced bushes with a symmetrical shape and three or four strong branches.

Blackberries and hybrid berries

Grow in sun or semi-shade. They can be grown against a fence or other framework, such as a wire support. Stretch four wires between strong posts 2m (6ft) high, driven firmly into the ground at either end

PLANTING A BUSH FRUIT

1 Clear the ground of weeds, including roots, and other debris. Then excavate the soil over an area at least twice the size of the rootball or container of the bush to allow for adequate soil improvement.

2 Although it is not essential, your fruit will do much better if you can add plenty of well-rotted manure or garden compost. Fork it into the bottom of the planting hole so that the roots are encouraged to grow down.

3 Soak the roots of bare-root plants in water for an hour before planting, and water container-grown plants at least half an hour before planting. Place the plant in the hole and use a cane to check it's at the right level.

4 Backfill with soil and firm the plant in well, pressing with the heel of the foot to remove any large pockets of air around the roots. Check the level before topping up with soil as necessary.

5 After firming the soil, hoe and rake the ground to remove footprints, taking care not to damage or disturb the stem. Water thoroughly and regularly until the canes are established.

6 Although it seems drastic, blackcurrant bushes are best cut back to about 23–30cm (9–12in) after planting. This will stimulate sturdy new shoots to grow from the base.

of the row. The wires should be 30cm (12in) apart, with the lowest wire 90cm (3ft) from the ground. Good blackberry varieties include 'Bedford Giant', 'Loch Ness' and 'Oregon Thornless'; hybrids include 'Tayberry' and 'Loganberry L654'. Look for strong, uniform blackberry canes that are at least pencil thickness, with no signs of shrivelling or pest and disease attack.

Gooseberries

Plant in a sunny position that's not exposed to strong winds. Space the bushes 1.5m (5ft) apart. You can also grow them as single-stemmed cordons spaced 30cm (1ft) apart against a wall or fence, or as a decorative standard. Good varieties include 'Invicta'. Choose well-balanced bushes with a symmetrical shape and four or five strong branches on a 10cm (4in) clean stem.

Raspberries

These also need a sunny site sheltered from strong winds. They can be grown in rows supported on wires. Stretch two wires between strong posts driven firmly into the ground either end of the row, the lower wire 90cm (3ft) above ground level, with the top wire at 1.5m (5ft). Plant 45cm (18in) apart along the row. Good varieties include 'Glen Moy', 'Glen Prosen', 'Malling Jewel', 'Malling Admiral' and 'Malling Leo'.

'Autumn Bliss' is a good autumn-fruiting variety. Look for strong, uniform canes that are at least pencil thickness, with no signs of disease.

Red and white currants

Plant in a sunny position sheltered from strong winds. They can be grown as bushes, cordons or fans spaced 1.8m (6ft), 1.2m (4ft) and 1.8m (6ft) apart respectively. Bushes or fans should be grown on a short stem ("leg"). Good red currant varieties include 'Laxton's No.1' and 'Red Lake'; good white currants include 'White Versailles'. Choose bushes with a symmetrical shape and three or four strong branches on a 10cm (4in) clean stem.

Pruning apples and pears

Late autumn is the ideal time to plant new trees and prune existing ones. If you are growing more than one tree, take into account both the rootstock and the pollination time. By choosing apple or pear varieties that blossom at the same time you can ensure a better set. Trees on dwarfing rootstocks can be planted 1.5m (5ft) apart, while trees on vigorous rootstocks should be spaced up to 7m (25ft) apart. The planting hole should be twice as wide and a little deeper than the rootball of the tree you are planting.

Pruning fruit trees

Despite a popular belief that apple and pear trees are difficult and time-consuming to keep in shape, if you buy trees that have been well trained, they will require the minimum of care. Apples and pears can be divided into two groups: some apple varieties produce fruit at the tips of their branches (known as tip bearers); while others and most pear varieties bear fruit on spurs produced on older wood. Most pruning involves the removal of dead or diseased wood, maintaining the overall shape and the thinning of fruiting spurs (see below).

Renovating neglected trees

If you leave a tree unpruned for a number of years it may well keep producing a good crop of fruit but they are likely to be variable in size and to be carried high up on the tree. Often, neglected trees will crop well in alternate years, producing a large crop of undersized fruit one year followed by a relatively lean year the next. If your tree answers this description, then late autumn is an ideal time to prune to put things right. Always start by cutting out any dead, diseased or dying branches.

Quick growth

Good vigour but little fruit is more often a problem with well-established young trees than old ones. Upright shoots are growing well and producing lots of leaf but few fruits. You could try summer pruning to

SPUR PRUNING AN APPLE BUSH TREE

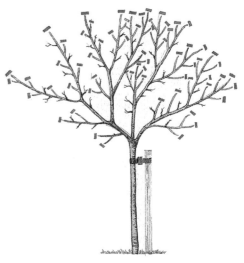

After planting, cut back the leader to about 75cm (30in) above the ground. Leave any side-shoots that appear just below this cut but remove any others lower down. The following year, reduce all new growth by about half. This will form the basic framework. Subsequent pruning is restricted to reducing the length of new growth by about a third and removing overcrowded growth.

When pruning pears, remove any dead, dying or weak growth, then remove crossing or very upright shoots, to leave a healthy tree of well-spaced branches.

help reduce the size and vigour, or you can use a technique called festooning, which requires no pruning at all. Simply tie all the whippy upright shoots down by their tips to hold them as near horizontal as possible – anchoring the end of each string to a sturdy stake. The sap in the stems will then be slowed and less upright growth and more blossom (and subsequently fruit) will be encouraged.

An older tree that makes a lot of growth often develops a thicket of crossing branches in the centre that prevent light getting in and encourage disease problems. Few fruits will be borne on these branches and any that are produced will be small and very late-ripening. Thin out any crossing branches, removing the weakest and least well positioned. Then remove any vertical shoots from the centre of the crown to open it up to light and air. Finally, step back from the tree and see if

PRUNING A DWARF PYRAMID PEAR

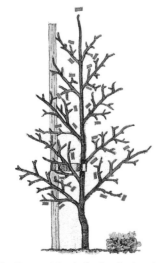

After planting, cut back the leader by about a third. Cut back the side shoots to about 15cm (6in). In the first summer, cut back the new growth on the main side of the shoots to about five leaves and on the secondary shoots to three leaves. Thereafter, cut back new growth on the main stems to five leaves and reduce other new growth to one leaf. During the winter, thin out any congested spurs.

A poorly pruned fruit tree will become less and less productive as the seasons pass and may not produce a crop at all.

there are any other branches that can be pruned back to help balance the shape of the canopy.

Neglected trees will often put all their vigour into the most vertical and highest branches. This means that the best fruit is often carried well out of reach at the top of the canopy. This can be a serious problem in a heavy cropping year, because these vertical branches tend to be weak and liable to break under a heavy load. All these problems can be overcome by shortening the main upright limbs back to a well-placed side branch lower down growing out at as near the horizontal as possible. Again, the aim is to end up with a lower canopy of well-spaced branches with an open centre.

Slow growth

Poor vigour and no fruit is usually associated with old, neglected trees that have practically stopped growing. You can increase the vigour and fruit production by pruning selected branches back by about a half to stimulate growth while maintaining the tree's overall shape. It may take several years before the tree is completely reinvigorated.

Pruning soft fruit

Soft fruit is generally simple to prune, mainly because all parts of the plant are within easy reach and the job can usually be done with secateurs (pruners). The aim, however, is the same as with tree fruit — to produce vigorous, healthy bushes and canes that bear good quality fruits year after year. As a matter of routine, always start by cutting out any dead, diseased or damaged stems.

Blackberries and hybrid berries

These fruit on one-year-old shoots, so after harvest, cut out all the fruited stems back to ground level. This will leave all the new shoots produced this year to fruit next year. If there are too many new shoots, thin out the weakest. Tie the remaining shoots to their support. If the plants have been allowed to get overgrown, you will have to wear thick, thornproof gloves and use a pair of long-handled pruners to cut out all but the new stems produced this year.

Blackcurrants

The best fruit is borne on one-year-old branches, so when pruning an established bush the aim is to remove the oldest shoots and encourage new ones. Prune while the plant is dormant. The easiest pruning method is to treat them the same way as many popular shrubs, using the one-in-three pruning method. Simply cut out one-third of the stems, starting with the oldest. This is the best method of rejuvenating an old, neglected plant because after three years' pruning all

Red currants fruit on old wood and can be grown as bushes or cordons, which are usually trained vertically.

PRUNING RASPBERRIES

1 Provided you are sure the variety is autumn-fruiting, simply cut all the canes down to ground level while they are dormant using a pair of secateurs (pruners).

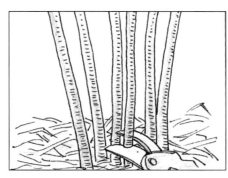

2 On summer-fruiting raspberries, cut the old canes (dark stems) that fruited this summer to just above the ground. Tie in the remaining shoots to support wires if necessary.

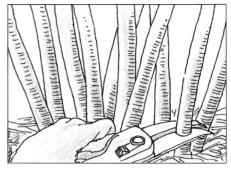

3 If the raspberries have been growing undisturbed for several years, the clumps may have become congested. Thin out surplus canes to be spaced about 8cm (3in) apart.

PRUNING BLACKCURRANTS

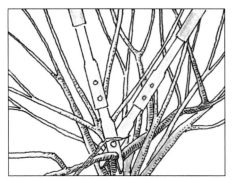

1 Cut back to their point of origin any diseased, damaged or badly placed shoots, leaving the strong, vigorous stems.

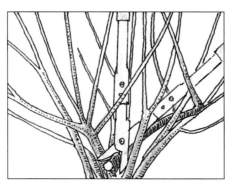

2 Start pruning only once the plants are old enough to fruit reliably. Cut back one-third of the oldest shoots close to the base.

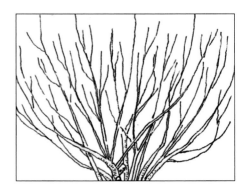

3 This is what the bush should look like after pruning, with plenty of well-spaced young shoots that will fruit next year.

PRUNING GOOSEBERRIES

1 If the job was not done after harvesting, cut back any low branches near the soil to an upward-pointing bud, and remove any badly placed and crossing branches. Try to ensure that the centre of the bush is left open.

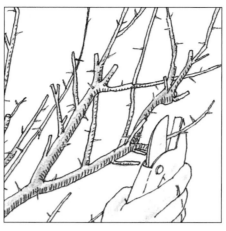

2 While the bush is dormant, reduce the length of new summer growth at the tips of the main shoots by about half. Then go along each main branch and prune back the side shoots to two buds from the old wood.

3 If the plant is old, cut out one or two of the oldest shoots, until you find a younger one to take over. You will need a pruning saw or loppers for the old wood. Thin the remainder for an open, well-balanced shape.

the stems will be young and vigorous. If you are short of time, pruning can be carried out at harvest time.

Gooseberries

These fruit on shoots that are a year or more old, and continue to fruit well even if you neglect pruning. But the spines on the stems make the fruit difficult to harvest unless the bush is pruned annually. The aim is to develop a well-balanced open shape – rather like a wine goblet, with well-spaced branches and an open centre. This also helps prevent gooseberry mildew, which can be a serious problem on congested bushes. You can bring an old, neglected bush back into shape by removing all the crossing shoots that congest the centre of the bush. Thin the rest to produce an open, well-balanced shape. This regime can also be carried out at harvest time.

Raspberries

Summer-fruiting raspberries fruit on shoots that are one year old. As soon as fruiting is over, loosen the canes from their support and cut all the fruited stems back down to ground level using a pair of secateurs. Tie in the most vigorous new canes to the support so that they are spaced 8cm (3in) apart, cutting out any surplus canes back to ground level. Make sure that all tall canes are securely fastened to the wires to prevent wind damage. This pruning can be carried out any time after fruiting.

Autumn-fruiting raspberries bear fruit on canes grown during the current year, so pruning is even easier. In this case, simply prune all the canes back to ground level after they have produced their fruit in the autumn.

Red and white currants

Unlike blackcurrants, these fruit on shoots that are at least two years old. The fruit-bearing shoots develop when the side shoots are pruned. The bushes are usually grown on a short length of clear stem (known as a "leg"), but can also be grown as bushes or trained as cordons. If pruning was not carried out in the summer, start by removing any crossing or overcrowded shoots, to allow light into the centre of the bush. Then shorten last summer's growth at the tip of each main shoot

by half. Finally, cut back the side shoots to within one or two buds of the main stem. This will encourage fruiting. On an old bush it may be necessary to cut out some of the older shoots that no longer fruit well, but try to leave a vigorous young side shoot to replace each one.

Gooseberries can be grown as bushes, cordons or standards. When pruning, aim to keep the centre of the plant as open as possible to encourage good air circulation when in leaf.

Winter

The onset of winter inevitably means fewer jobs to do in the garden, and most of your time will be spent digging and tidying up the vegetable plot. This is also a good time for taking a critical look at how you can improve your soil in time for the next growing season. Most types of soil benefit from the addition of well-rotted organic matter. This fibrous material acts like a sponge in light, sandy soils to make them better able to hold on to moisture, while in clay soils it introduces air pockets, opening up the soil structure and allowing water to drain more freely. It is, therefore, worth adding as much well-rotted manure, garden compost, composted bark or spent mushroom compost as you can. Midwinter is the time for mainly indoor jobs, such as planning for the year ahead and ordering seeds and plants. By late winter you can sow the first seeds in the greenhouse, and outdoors start warming up the soil with cloches. This will enable you to give your vegetables a head start in early spring.

Established rhubarb crowns can be lifted and forced to provide a succulent crop in late winter.

Knowing your soil

The type of soil you have in your garden will have a great influence on the way you garden and on what types of vegetables and fruit grow best. It is useful, therefore, to get to know what your soil is like from the outset. That way, you are likely to make fewer mistakes. You can, of course, learn quite a lot by looking at what is already growing well in your own garden and in your neighbours' plots.

Soil structure

Seeing whether drought-loving plants or water-hungry plants such as beans are happy in your garden will be a guide to the type of soil you have. You can also learn a lot by feeling the texture. Wet a small lump of soil and rub it between finger and thumb. If it feels slippery and slimy the soil probably contains a lot of clay particles, if it is gritty then sand is predominant. If it is neither, it is probably a balanced mixture of sand, silt and clay, known as a loamy soil.

Clay soils The tiny particles in clay soils will compact, especially when walked on, so that water cannot drain away and air cannot penetrate. In spring clay soils tend to be cold and wet and are difficult to work. In summer they can dry out to form solid lumps. However, the water retention means clay soils are generally fertile.

Sandy soils The particles in sandy soil are mainly much larger and of an irregular shape, so do not pack down, resulting in lots of air pockets that allow water to drain freely through the soil. This means that nutrients are easily washed out (known as leaching). In spring sandy soils are easy to work and tend to warm up quickly, but in summer they often dry out.

Silty soils With particle sizes between those of clay and sand, silty soils are generally free-draining but hold on to moisture better than sandy soils. However, unlike sandy soils they are easily compacted if walked on when wet.

TAKING A pH TEST

1 Place the soil in the test tube until it reaches the mark on the side.

2 Put a layer of barium sulphate powder into the tube level with the mark. This compound helps the solution to clear rapidly and makes the pH reading clearer.

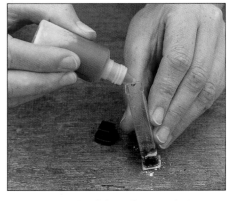

3 Pour in a little of the indicator solution up to the mark shown on the tube. Be careful not to put in too much because this can make the solution dark and difficult to read.

4 Add distilled water to the mark on the tube, put the lid on and shake the container vigorously for about a minute. Leave the contents to settle.

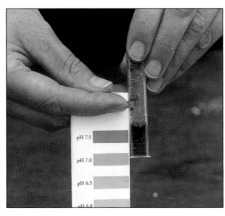

5 Once sufficiently cleared, compare the colour with those on the chart, choosing the one that most closely matches that of the solution.

If you find your soil is too acid for the plants you want to grow, you can reduce the acidity by adding lime some weeks before planting.

TAKING A NUTRIENT TEST

1 Place a small sample of the soil into the test tube up to the mark on the side.

2 Add a test solution (in this case one for nitrogen) up to the mark on the test tube.

3 Filter the solution to remove soil particles and leave just a liquid solution.

4 Decant the resulting filtered solution into another container for the final stage of the nutrient test.

5 Add a small amount of indicator powder. This will react with the solution and enable a colour reading to be taken.

6 Shake for about 10 seconds and compare with the chart. Here, the reading indicates that a nitrogen-rich fertilizer will benefit this soil.

Loam soils These soils tend to contain a balanced mixture of clay, sand and silt, providing the perfect conditions for plant growth heavygood cropping: free-draining but moisture-retentive and fertile. They warm up quickly in spring and do not dry out too much in summer. This is the type of soil to which most gardeners aspire.

Acid or alkaline?

The other factor you need to know when choosing plants for your garden is how acid or alkaline your soil is. This is measured on a pH scale ranging from 1 to 14, although the extremes are rarely encountered. The mid-point (7) is neutral and anything higher is progressively more alkaline, while anything lower is progressively more acid. Most plants prefer a pH of about 6.5, slightly on the acid side of neutral. Some plants need acid soil, of pH 5.5–6, while others need more alkaline conditions.

Testing your soil

Many people garden successfully without ever testing their soil, but they are probably fortunate in gardening on ground that is not deficient in nutrients, is neither too acid nor too alkaline, and receives plenty of nutrients as part of normal cultivation.

   If plants don't seem to be growing well, take a soil test. Professional soil testing is the most accurate for nutrients, but you can get a reasonable idea of the major nutrients in your soil with simple indicator kits. Testing for pH is quick and effective, but bear in mind that kits can vary from one manufacturer to another, so always follow the instructions if they are different from the advice given here.

IMPROVING SOIL FERTILITY

The fertility of the soil is much improved by the addition of organic material, but a quick boost can also be achieved by adding a proprietary fertilizer, spreading it over the surface and then raking it in.

Improving your soil

Fortunately, you don't need to know what type of soil you have to make improvements, because they all benefit from the addition of well-rotted organic matter. Unless you have a very peaty soil (which is already rich in organic matter) it is worth adding as much manure and garden compost as you can. All good gardeners make their own compost, because this is the best soil-improving material there is.

Adding organic matter

Organic matter can be dug into the soil or applied as a mulch and left for worms to take it down. It acts like a sponge in light, sandy soils, helping them retain moisture, while in clay soils it opens up the structure and improves drainage.

It will also improve the fertility of poor soils because it releases nutrients as it is broken down by soil-borne organisms. It is important that the organic matter is well-rotted before it is added to the soil; otherwise it will continue to break down in the soil, using up valuable nitrogen in the process. Another way to add organic material is by growing green manures: nutritious, quick-growing crops that are sown on vacant ground and then dug in, to rot down in the soil.

SINGLE DIGGING

1 Divide the space in half lengthways. Mark the area with string. This avoids moving soil from one end of the plot to the other.

2 Take out a trench the depth and width of a single spade blade. Pile the soil at the end of the other half of the plot, as shown.

3 When you remove the next trench, throw the soil forward into the space left by the first. Digging is easier if you first "cut" a slice with the spade right across the plot.

4 Push the spade in parallel to the end of the trench, taking a slice of soil about 15–20cm (6–8in) deep. Larger bites may be too heavy to lift comfortably.

5 Loosen the soil by pulling back on the handle, while aiming to keep the bite of soil on the spade. Keeping the spade upright places less strain on your back.

6 Flick the soil over with the wrist, inverting the clod of earth so that the top is buried. Lift the weight with your knees, not your back.

7 When the end of the plot is reached, fill the trench with the soil you took from the first row of the return strip.

8 Finally, fill the trench left when all the digging has been completed with the soil put on one side from the initial excavation.

When to dig

If you have a vegetable plot or other large area of ground that requires digging, this is a good time of year to do it. If the soil is a heavy clay, leaving it rough-dug over the winter will allow the action of frost and the weather to help break down large clods. This will make it easier to rake level and to produce a seedbed of tilth, a fine, crumbly soil, in spring. You may prefer to leave digging a light, sandy soil until spring, because this type of soil tends to become flattened and compacted by winter rain if dug too early. New weed growth may also be a problem by spring and can be dealt with at the same time.

How to dig

Recently cultivated soil or small areas between plants can be dug most easily using a garden fork. Push in the fork to the full length of its tines and turn over the soil, breaking down any clods as you go. Incorporate well-rotted organic matter, or lay it on the surface as a mulch for soil-borne organisms such as earthworms to do the work for you. Vacant ground is probably best dug over with a spade. There are three main methods to choose from: simple, single and double digging – although there are many variations of each.

Simple digging is a quick and easy way of cultivating lighter soils. The

Green manures

Broad (fava) beans	nitrogen fixing
Italian ryegrass	quick growing
Lupins	nitrogen fixing
Mustard	quick growing
Phacelia	quick growing
Red clover	nitrogen fixing
Winter tare	nitrogen fixing

DOUBLE DIGGING

1 Divide the plot up in the same way as described for single digging, and deal with the soil from the end of each strip in the same way. But this time make the trenches about 40cm (16in) wide and 25cm (10in) deep.

2 Spread a generous layer of well-rotted manure or garden compost – or other bulky organic material that will retain moisture and add humus – over the bottom of the trench.

3 Fork this thick layer of manure or organic material into the bottom of the trench. A fork is better than a spade because it will penetrate the harder lower layer more easily and will mix the material into the soil better.

4 Move the garden line to the next position, maintaining the same 40cm (16in) spacing, or thereabouts. Cut and slice the soil and throw it forward as before, but take several bites per strip, so that the volume of soil isn't too heavy.

blade of the spade is pushed into the ground vertically and the handle is eased back to loosen the soil. The spade is turned and lifted in one motion to invert the spadeful of soil in the same hole it came from. This is a useful way of burying organic matter laid on the surface.

On heavier soils, single digging (see opposite) is a better technique for incorporating organic matter into the surface layer of the soil, and is likely to do more good for short-rooted plants than burying it deeply. However, for certain deep-rooted crops, such as runner beans, or to break up neglected ground, double digging (see above) can be useful.

ROTAVATING

In larger gardens with heavy soil, a rotavator (rototiller) will break down the soil into a fine tilth. Even a small one saves a lot of time, especially if the soil is too dry to break down with a rake.

Forcing winter crops

With a little forward planning, you can get home-grown rhubarb and forced chicory as early as late winter. The traditional technique of forcing was widely used before the invention of domestic freezers, but even though we can now store a wide range of vegetables, as well as buying imported produce, it is highly satisfying to be able to pick some fresh crops from the garden in winter.

Practical matters

You will need to give the plants a period of cold so that they will grow vigorously when they are placed in a warmer environment. If you grow them in total darkness you will get fast and tender growth. It will be about six weeks before you can pull

your first crop of rhubarb and half this time for chicory. You can force rhubarb and chicory outdoors too, but you will have a longer wait. Rhubarb crops will be ready for pulling from early spring and chicory from late winter.

Rhubarb

This is one of those crops that almost looks after itself, and if you have an established clump, forcing tender young stems is very easy. There are many methods of forcing rhubarb, and they all seem to work well. Just choose a technique that you find convenient. You need a method of excluding light. Special jars were once used for this, but now most people improvise. An old tea chest, bucket or barrel are simple but

effective alternatives. If you don't have these, make a frame from wire-netting and canes as shown here. Pile straw into the wire-netting cage, pressing it down firmly, to provide warmth and protection. Another simple way to make a rhubarb forcer is with a plastic dustbin (trash can). If you don't mind cutting the bottom out of it, use it the right way up with a lid on; otherwise use it inverted without a lid.

For really early crops many gardeners lift a well-established root and leave this on the surface for a few weeks. This gives the root a cold spell that makes it think winter is more advanced than it is. Replant your chilled crown for outdoor forcing or bring it into the greenhouse. If you have a warm greenhouse, place it under the bench, screened with black plastic. Alternatively, pot it up and put in a plastic bag to take indoors. Make sure there is plenty of air in the bag by keeping it loose and making a few small air holes, then place the bag in a warm place – under the stairs or in a kitchen cupboard. Check progress from time to time.

Chicory

Chicons, the forced and blanched new shoots produced from chicory roots, are an enjoyable winter

> ### Writing labels in advance
>
> It makes sense to do as many jobs as you can in winter that will save time later when you are busy sowing and planting. Instead of waiting, write your labels on a day when you can't get into the garden. You will probably make a neater job of it by doing it at leisure, and it will take pressure off the time when you're busy in the garden.

Lift well-established rhubarb crowns and leave on the surface for a few weeks before forcing indoors.

vegetable when fresh produce is scarce. It is best if you grow your own roots from plants sown in late spring or early summer, but you may be able to buy roots for forcing. Outdoors, leave the chicory roots in situ, cutting the foliage off in late autumn. Heap soil over the stumps, creating a ridge 20cm (8in) high. Place cloches over the top and insulate on cold nights, removing the insulation during mild, sunny days to allow the sun's rays to warm the soil through the cloches. You should check the roots in late winter to see whether they are ready to cut.

FORCING RHUBARB

1 Choose a method of excluding light. Special pots were once used for this, but now most people improvise. An old tea chest, bucket, or barrel are simple but effective alternatives. If you don't have these, make a frame from wire-netting and canes as shown here.

2 Pile straw into the wire-netting cage, pressing it well down, to provide warmth and protection.

3 Another simple way to make a rhubarb forcer is with a plastic dustbin (trash can). If you don't mind cutting the bottom out of it, use it the right way up with a lid on, otherwise use it inverted without a lid.

4 For really early crops many gardeners lift a well-established root to leave on the surface for a few weeks. This gives the root a cold spell that makes it think winter is more advanced than it is.

5 Replant your chilled crown for outdoor forcing, or pot it up and bring it into a heated greenhouse, or a warm place in the house. Wrap it loosely in black plastic to exclude light, and check progress regularly.

FORCING CHICORY

1 To produce chicons you should choose a variety of chicory recommended for the purpose, such as 'Witloof', an old variety. Lift the root from mid-autumn onwards, and leave it on the soil surface for a few days.

2 When the roots have been exposed for a few days, which helps to retard growth, trim the tops to leave a 2.5–5cm (1–2in) stump of growth. You can pot them up or store them in a box of sand, peat or dry soil for use later.

3 Pot up three roots and cover the pot with a second pot with the drainage holes blocked. Keep at a temperature of 10–18°C (50–65°F), with the compost (soil mix) just moist. The chicons will be ready in about three weeks.

Warming up the soil

In the vegetable garden, start warming up the soil in late winter with cloches or mulches to get your vegetables off to an early start. Although most early vegetables are not sown until early spring, you need to have your cloches in position several weeks before you plan to sow. This effectively lengthens the growing season and provides early crops for the table.

Using a coldframe

If your coldframe is not packed with overwintering plants, make use of it now for early vegetable crops. Radishes and turnips are among the crops that grow quickly and mature early in a coldframe, but you can also try forcing varieties of carrot. Some varieties of lettuce also do well. Dig over the ground in the frame, working in as much organic material as possible. Well-rotted farmyard manure that has been put through a sieve is useful for enriching the soil for these early crops. Do not apply powerful artificial fertilizers at this time. Rake the soil level, and make shallow drills with your rake or a hoe. You can sow the seeds broadcast (scattered randomly), but this makes weeding and thinning more difficult.

Sow early peas and beans now in containers to get them off to a flying start.

Sow the seeds thinly, then rake the soil back over the drills. Water thoroughly, then keep the frame closed until the seeds germinate. Once they are through, ventilate on mild days, but keep closed, and if possible insulated, at night, especially when frost is forecast.

Prepare for beans and celery

You can grow a satisfactory crop of beans without taking special steps to improve the soil and achieve a fairly respectable crop of self-blanching celery by planting on ground that has not been specially enriched. But if you want an especially heavy and impressive crop, it is worth preparing the trench thoroughly first.

Take out a trench 25–30cm (10–12in) deep and 60cm (2ft) wide for runner beans, or 38cm (15in) wide for celery. Heap the soil to one side or both sides of the trench. Add as much well-rotted manure or garden compost as you can spare. This will add some nutrients and improve the structure and moisture-holding capacity of the soil. Fork the manure or compost into the soil at the bottom of the trench — don't leave it as a layer. Finally, rake the excavated soil back into the trench.

Early peas and beans

Peas and beans germinate readily in warm soil in early spring, but you can get them off to a flying start now by sowing in pots or in a length of gutter indoors (see below). This is also a useful technique for keeping sowings on schedule if you garden on heavy soil that is slow to warm up in spring, or if the weather is particularly cold or wet.

SOWING PEAS IN GUTTERING

1 A length of plastic guttering is ideal for starting off pea seeds early in the season. Block the ends and fill with soil.

2 Sow the seeds about 5–8cm (2–3in) apart, cover with soil, then keep warm and moist. Harden off the plants when ready to plant out.

3 Take out a drill with a draw hoe, and gradually slide the peas out of the gutter and into the row so that you do not disturb them.

WARMING A SEEDBED

1 Cloche designs vary considerably, but most can easily be made into long runs the length of the row. Make sure that they are butted close together and that plastic cloches are well anchored to the ground.

2 End pieces are essential for rigid cloches, otherwise they will just become a wind tunnel, which will be unsuitable for plants. Make sure they are fixed firmly in place with stakes or special clips.

3 Sheet plastic tunnel cloches are inexpensive to buy, and although they need to be re-covered after a few seasons, a replacement sheet is inexpensive. Fix the hoops first, then stretch the sheet over them.

4 Use the special fixing wires to hold the sheet in position so it does not blow away.

5 Secure the ends with sticks or pegs, pulling the plastic taut and fastening it down.

6 Heap a little soil over the edges to anchor the cloche and stop wind lifting the sides.

Well chitted potatoes have several short sturdy shoots and are ready for planting.

Chitting potato tubers

The technique known as chitting simply means encouraging the potato tubers to sprout before planting. It is useful if you want the tubers to get off to a quick start, as they will usually be through the ground a week or two before unchitted tubers. Maincrop potatoes can be treated in the same way but it is not really necessary. Place the tubers in a tray in a light position, perhaps by a window, where there is no risk of frost. The kind of long shoots that appear when potatoes have been stored in the dark for some time are no use – the shoots must be short and sturdy. Planting is easiest when they are about 2cm (¾in) long, which usually takes about six weeks.

Apply slow-acting fertilizers

Apply slow-acting fertilizers, such as bonemeal and proprietary controlled-release fertilizers, when the vegetable plot has been dug and levelled, prior to sowing from early spring onwards.

Controlled-release fertilizers release their nutrients only when the soil is warm enough for the plants to use them. Fertilizers should always be applied evenly and at the rate recommended by the manufacturer.

Divide the area into strips 1m (1yd) wide with string, and space canes at the same interval to form a square. Sprinkle the measured dose, then move the canes to form the next 1m (1yd) square down the row. Repeat until the whole area has been treated. Rake the fertilizer into the soil.

Jobs in Brief: Spring

In cold regions the weather can still be icy in early spring, but in mild climates you can make a start on many outdoor jobs. If sowing or planting outdoors, bear in mind that soil temperature as well as air temperature is important. Few seeds will germinate if the soil temperature is below 7°C (45°F), so use a soil thermometer to check before you sow. Many more sowings can be made in the greenhouse.

SPRING JOBS IN BRIEF

Early spring
- [ ] Prepare the vegetable plot by applying fertilizer
- [ ] Protect early crops with garden fleece
- [ ] Start sowing vegetables without protection if you live in a mild area
- [ ] Plant onion sets
- [ ] Make a herb wheel
- [ ] Divide herbaceous herbs, such as chives
- [ ] Sow hardier vegetables in trays or pots in the greenhouse
- [ ] Prick out seedlings

Mid spring
- [ ] Prepare the soil for seeds
- [ ] Start sowing vegetables that do not need protection
- [ ] Improve areas of stony soil
- [ ] Plant potatoes
- [ ] Transplant cabbages and cauliflowers
- [ ] Protect crops against light frosts
- [ ] Put cloches over strawberries if you want an early crop
- [ ] Protect crops against pests
- [ ] Plant a herb garden
- [ ] Sow tender vegetables in the greenhouse.

Late spring
- [ ] Sow corn outdoors
- [ ] Thin seedlings
- [ ] Plant tender crops
- [ ] Plant runner and pole beans
- [ ] Harvest early crops
- [ ] Earth (hill) up potatoes
- [ ] Stake and pinch out beans
- [ ] Plant up a herb pot
- [ ] Control mint
- [ ] Keep your greenhouse cool by opening vents, providing shading and spraying water over the floor
- [ ] Plant or prick out greenhouse tomatoes and cucumbers

Plant onion sets by pulling the soil back over the drill, to leave the tips of the onions protruding. If birds are a problem – they may try to pull the onions out by the wispy old stems – protect with netting.

If you want an early crop, cover strawberries with cloches, but remember to leave access for pollinating insects when the plants are in flower. Most cloches will have a system of ventilation that allows for this on warm days.

If you use canes to support runner beans, a wigwam shape makes a good framework. Plant the beans just to one side of each cane. Tie them to the canes as soon as they are tall enough and continue to tie them in.

Jobs in Brief: Summer

Now is the time to harvest your crops: early potatoes, broad (fava) beans, peas, spinach, cabbage and carrots, followed later in the summer by French (green) and runner beans, courgettes (zucchini), onions and corn.

Harvest fruit as it ripens and prepare it for storing. The main tasks during the summer months will be feeding and watering, dealing with pests and diseases, and keeping the weeds at bay.

SUMMER JOBS IN BRIEF

Early summer
- [ ] Water vegetables
- [ ] Control weeds
- [ ] Plant late potatoes
- [ ] Harvest early vegetables
- [ ] Prune fruit such plums, cherries and apricots
- [ ] Layer blackberries and cut back strawberries
- [ ] Sow French beans
- [ ] Spray aphids on broad beans and root flies on cabbages, carrots and onions
- [ ] Feed and water greenhouse crops and try biological pest control

Midsummer
- [ ] Grow and train vegetables – earth up leeks, trim outdoor tomatoes, blanch celery, protect cauliflowers
- [ ] Harvest herbs regularly
- [ ] Dry herbs for winter use: store herbs away from direct sunlight
- [ ] Summer prune cordon and espalier apples
- [ ] Give plants that need a boost a dressing dose of quick-acting fertilizer, and if using a powder or granules be sure to water in thoroughly
- [ ] Keep a check on weeds

Late summer
- [ ] Ripen and harvest onions
- [ ] Harvest other vegetables, such as aubergines (eggplants), courgettes), French beans, potatoes, corn and turnips
- [ ] Choose a suitable way of storing vegetables
- [ ] Harvest fruit in prime condition, taking care not to damage it as this will make it rot later on
- [ ] Choose a suitable way of storing fruit – freezing, storing in trays or cooking and preserving are some of the alternatives

Avoid wasting water by laying a seep or drip hose along a row of strawberries or other plants. In this way only the immediate area will be watered as the water slowly seeps out of the pipe and soaks into the ground.

It is never possible to eliminate weeds entirely, but you should try to keep them under control because they rob the soil of nutrients. You should always avoid using chemical weedkillers near fruit, vegetables or herbs.

As soon as the foliage of onions has turned a straw colour and is brittle, lift them with a fork and leave them on the surface for a few days to dry off. Lay the onions with the roots facing the sun.

Jobs in Brief: Autumn

The weather in early autumn is still warm enough to make outdoor gardening a comfortable experience, but it's a good idea to protect outdoor tomatoes and lettuce. By mid-autumn you will also need to protect Swiss chard, and pot up some herbs for use during the winter. Now is the time to tidy up the garden ready for winter and to add organic material to the soil. Fallen leaves will be plentiful, and small quantities can be added to the compost heap, but they tend to rot down more slowly than other waste so don't add too many.

AUTUMN JOBS IN BRIEF

Early autumn
- [ ] Protect outdoor tomatoes with cloches or fleece to extend their season and ripen more fruit
- [ ] Place cloches over lettuces and other low-growing vegetables
- [ ] Cut down asparagus haulms and apply a mulch
- [ ] Plant garlic
- [ ] Store vegetables

Mid-autumn
- [ ] Pot up herbs for winter use
- [ ] Use cloches or coldframes to protect Swiss chard
- [ ] Cut back globe artichokes
- [ ] Harvest leeks
- [ ] Add organic material such as well-rotted garden compost, farmyard manure, composted bark or spent mushroom compost

Late autumn
- [ ] Plan a soft fruit garden – a sunny site that is sheltered from cold winds is ideal
- [ ] Plant bush fruit
- [ ] Support cane fruit
- [ ] Prune apples and pears
- [ ] Renovate neglected trees
- [ ] Prune blackcurrants, gooseberries and raspberries

Lift potatoes with a fork once the foliage has died down (top). Leave the tubers on the surface for a couple of hours so that the skins dry off and harden. Sort the potatoes before storing them. Grade them into four sizes: very small, small, medium and large (above).

Chives respond well to lifting for an extended season. Use a fork to lift a small clump complete with rootball and soil to pot up. Move the pot into the greehouse, where the chives will remain productive long after those outside in the garden have died back.

Most trees can be planted at any time of the year but they will establish more quickly if planted in the autumn as this is when the soil is moist and still warm. Bare-root trees are only available to buy in the garden centre when they are dormant.

Jobs in brief: Winter

If you made an early start with winter jobs like digging and adding organic matter to the vegetable plot, mid-winter is a time mainly for indoor jobs such as ordering seeds and plants. By attending to these in good time you are more likely to make the right decisions and have everything ready for late winter and early spring when gardening begins again in earnest. By late winter you can start sowing seeds in the greenhouse or propagators.

WINTER JOBS IN BRIEF

Early winter
- [ ] Test your soil
- [ ] Apply lime to your soil if the test shows it is necessary
- [ ] Make a nutrient test
- [ ] Improve soil fertility by adding some organic material or for a quick boost add a proprietary fertilizer
- [ ] Incorporate organic matter into the surface layer of the soil by single digging
- [ ] For certain deep-rooted crop, such as runner beans or to break up neglected ground, double dig
- [ ] Break down heavy soil into a fine tilth using a rotavator

Midwinter
- [ ] Force rhubarb
- [ ] Write labels in advance
- [ ] Force chicory
- [ ] Place cloches over the top of chicory and insulate on cold nights

Late winter
- [ ] Finish winter digging
- [ ] Apply slow-acting fertilizers when the vegetable plot has been dug and levelled
- [ ] Force rhubarb
- [ ] Start warming up the soil with floating cloches or mulches to get vegetables off to a good start in the spring
- [ ] Sow peas and beans in pots or in a length of gutter indoors
- [ ] Sow early crops in coldframes or beneath cloches
- [ ] Prepare runner bean and celery trenches
- [ ] Chit "seed" potatoes (small tubers) of early varieties

If you have a large garden with heavy clay soil, consider buying a rotavator (rototiller), which will make breaking down the soil into a fine tilth much easier. Even a small one saves a lot of time and effort, especially if the soil is too dry to break down with a rake.

There are many different ways to force rhubarb – make a frame from wire netting and fill with straw (top) or use a plastic dustbin (trash can) and cut the bottom out, using it the right way up with a lid on, or use it inverted without a lid.

Cloches are made of different materials and designs vary considerably, but most can be easily made into long runs the length of a row. Make sure that they are butted close together and are well anchored to prevent strong winds blowing them away.

Glossary

Bare-root A plant sold with no soil or compost around the roots. They are dug up from the nursery field and are ready for planting in the dormant season.

Biological control The use of a pest's natural enemies to control its numbers in the garden or greenhouse.

Capillary matting An absorbent material that holds a lot of water on which containers are placed and from which they can draw all the moisture they need.

Certified stock Plants that have been inspected and declared free of specific pests and diseases. They can be used as stock plants for propagation material.

Chit A technique used to encourage a potato tuber to begin to sprout before planting.

Cloche A small structure made from glass, clear plastic or polythene that is used to warm small areas of soil or protect vulnerable plants.

Compost (soil mix) A mixture used for growing plants in containers. It can be loam-based or peat-based. Peat-free versions are now available based on coir, composted bark or other organic waste material.

Compost, garden A material that has been produced from the decomposition of organic waste material in a compost bin or heap. Useful as a soil improver or planting mixture.

Cordon A trained form of tree or bush with a main stem, vertical or at an angle, and with side shoots shortened to form fruiting spurs.

Crop covers Various porous materials used to protect plants or crops. Horticultural fleece protects plants from frost and flying insect pests; insect-proof mesh is a well-ventilated fabric, ideal for keeping out insects throughout the summer, but offers no frost protection.

Cultivate To prepare the land and soil for growing crops.

Damping down Wetting surfaces in a greenhouse to raise air humidity and to help keep temperatures down.

Earth (hill) up To draw up soil around a plant forming a mound. Potatoes are earthed up to protect new shoots from frost and to prevent tubers from being exposed to light.

Espalier A trained form of tree or bush where the main stem is vertical and pairs of side shoots are at a set spacing and trained out horizontally.

Fan A trained form of tree or bush where the main stem is vertical and pairs of side shoots are pruned at set spacing and trained out at either side to form a fan shape.

Fleece *see* Crop covers

Grafted plant A plant that has been attached on to the rootstock of another variety. Trees, especially fruit trees, are often grafted on to dwarfing rootstocks, while ornamental plants may be grafted on to a more vigorous variety.

Hardening off A method of gradually weaning a plant from the conditions inside to those outside without causing a check to growth.

Hardiness The amount of cold a type of plant is able to withstand. Hardy plants can tolerate frost; half-hardy and tender plants cannot.

Horticultural fleece *see* Crop covers

Humus The organic residue of decayed organic matter found in soil. It improves soil fertility.

Insect-proof mesh *see* Crop covers

Leafmould A material that has been produced from the decomposition of leaves in a leaf bin or heap. Useful as a soil improver or planting mixture.

Manure A bulky organic animal waste that is rotted down and used to improve soil structure and fertility.

Mulch A material that is laid on the surface of the soil to prevent moisture loss through

evaporation and suppress weed growth. A mulch can be loose and organic, such as composted bark or garden compost, loose and inorganic, such as gravel, or a fabric, such as mulch matting or landscape fabric.

Pricking out The spacing of seedlings while still small so that they have room to develop and grow on.

Rootball A mass of roots and compost that holds together when a plant is removed from its container.

Runner A horizontal shoot that spreads out from the plant, roots and forms another plant.

Slow-release fertilizer A specially coated inorganic fertilizer that releases its nutrients slowly.

Sucker A shoot that arises from the roots underground. The term is usually applied to shoots from the rootstock of a grafted plant that has different characteristics to the growing variety.

Transplanting The transfer of seedlings or young plants from a nursery bed where they were sown to their final growing position.

Windbreak A hedge, fence, wall or fabric that is used to filter the wind and therefore reduce the damage that it may cause.

Index